Motorcycle Journeys Through the

by John Hermann

A Whirlaway Book
Whitehorse Press, Boston

A Whirlaway Book. Published August 1993 by
    Whitehorse Press
    154 West Brookline Street
    Boston, Massachusetts 02118, U.S.A.

Whirlaway and Whitehorse Press are trademarks of
Kennedy Associates.

ISBN 0-9621834-6-6

5 4 3 2 1

Printed in the United States of America

Dedication

All these roads have been discovered and enjoyed and played on and replayed on with such a wondrous company of friends as any person could hope for.

To ride the roads again, or to write of riding them, or to read of riding them, is to recall those good friends with whom they've been shared. Indelibly etched on my mind with each hairpin, each view, each culinary delight, is the memory of good friends who were there with me. To them, with the hope that they too remember, I would like to dedicate this book.

Until we ride again in the Alps.

WARNING!

Alpine roads and scenery and culture are known to cause Alpinitis, a disease that creates an almost uncontrollable urge to return. There is no cure. The only relief is more Alpine riding, which results in reinfection.

Contents

Motorcycle Journeys Through the Alps

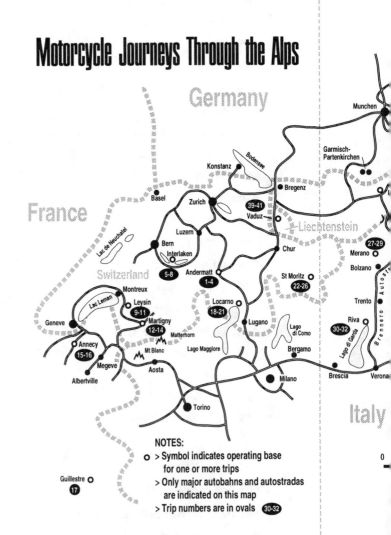

Germany

Munchen

Garmisch-
Partenkirchen

Konstanz

Bodensee

Bregenz

France

Basel

Zurich

39-41

Vaduz

Liechtenstein

Merano

27-29

Luzern

Bern

Interlaken

Chur

Bolzano

Switzerland

5-8

Andermatt

1-4

St Moritz

22-26

Lac de Neuchatel

Montreux

Leysin

9-11

Locarno

18-21

Trento

Lac Leman

Geneve

Martigny

12-14

Matterhorn

Lugano

Lago
di Como

Riva

30-32

Lago di Garda

Brennero Autostr

Annecy

15-16

Mt Blanc

Lago Magglore

Bergamo

Megeve

Aosta

Brescia

Verona

Albertville

Milano

Torino

Italy

NOTES:

○ > Symbol indicates operating base
  for one or more trips

> Only major autobahns and autostradas
  are indicated on this map

Guillestre ○

17

> Trip numbers are in ovals 30-32

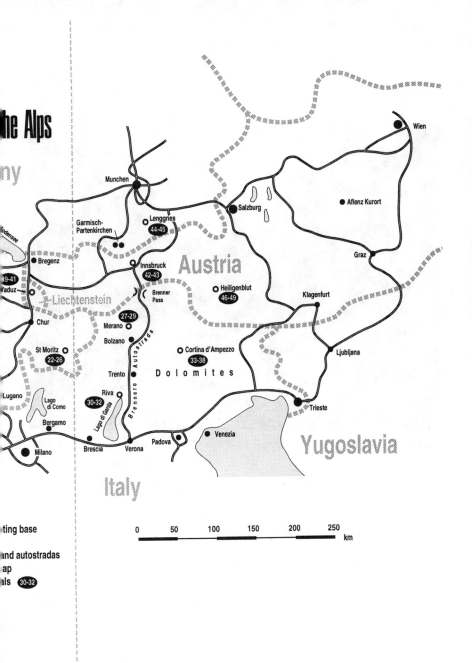

he Alps

ny

Bodensee

Wien

Munchen

Salzburg

Aflenz Kurort

Garmisch-
Partenkirchen

Lenggries
44-45

Bregenz

Graz

49-41

Innsbruck
42-43

Austria

Waduz

Liechtenstein

Brenner
Pass

Heiligenblut
46-49

Klagenfurt

Chur

Merano

27-29

St Moritz

22-26

Bolzano

Cortina d'Ampezzo
33-38

Ljubljana

Trento

D o l o m i t e s

Lugano

Riva

30-32

Lago
di Como

Trieste

Bergamo

Lago di Garda

Brennero   Autostrada

Padova

Venezia

Yugoslavia

Milano

Brescia

Verona

Italy

ting base

0   50   100   150   200   250

km

nd autostradas

ap

ls 30-32

Here, several riders carve their way down Passo della Stelvio in Italy. On Alpine roads there are no double yellows. You get no more road than you need, or can claim.

Foreword

Two years riding in the Alps. Actually, I've ridden in the Alps a little more than two years worth of days during the past decade or so, exploring each little road and pass, checking out motorcycle favorites, all in 26 trips of three to five weeks each. Some rain, some fog, some sleet, some snow—but more sunshine and lots of fun and friends.

So I've more experience riding than writing. But writing seems to be a good way to pass on some of the things I've learned. I hope this book will encourage you to explore and enjoy the Alps. Not only do I point you to the good roads, I hope to ease concern about things that might take trial and error and time and money to discover.

In writing, I find that I'm a bit uncomfortable using the first person: "I took this road," or "I recommend that souffle," or "I had the corner room with a view." My intention is that, except for this Foreword, I will seldom use the first person. The second person 'you' also bothers me, as it seems to separate me from you. Rather, I imagine that we're traveling together, or at least talking together, and I try to write as if we were discussing the roads and circumstances.

You should know that the maps don't always agree on the spelling of place names. Italian maps have their opinion, German maps insist on theirs, etc. Are Swiss maps a good compromise? I lean toward Kummerly and Frey, although I also use maps by Kompass, Freytag and Borndt, Verlag, RV, Studio F.M.B., Hallwag, and Michelin. I've tried verifying in the field, but road signs are often abbreviated, and sometimes I just forgot. To give you an example of the problem, I have two Austrian maps, printed in Austria. One says Solker Pass, one says Solk Pass. The Italian map calls it Solker. So do I. Some maps say Passo dello Stelvio, some say Passo di Stelvio.

Here are some assumptions I've made while writing:

- German nouns are almost always capitalized. Italian and French nouns are capitalized, as in English, when they are the name of something. For example, Pass is always capitalized if it's German, but the French equivalent, col, and the Italian, passo, only when they're part of a name.
- I lean toward Anglicizing plurals of a few German and Italian words. The plural of the German word, Autobahn is Autobahnen. I say Autobahns. The plural of Italian

autostrada is autostrade. I say autostradas. Gelato, gelati, gelaterias. You get the idea. What I have written may not be completely correct linguistically, but I have tried to capture the international flavor while keeping the words familiar to other Americans.

- In the text, there will be no German umlauts or French accent marks. Their chief function is to guide pronunciation. There are some phonetic aids in the text.
- The French don't use the d' or l' in alphabetizing place names. In our index, L'Isere River is under I, not L.
- St. is the abbreviation for Saint in French and Sankt in German. (It's Sankt Moritz.) Rather than make that distinction, I put both French and German saints alphabetically under "St." in the index.

I start the book at Andermatt, Switzerland, in the very middle of the Alps, a very good place to start a book or a trip. Then, in what I hope is an orderly and reasonable fashion, I describe every road and some facilities to the west, then to the south, and, finally, to the east of Andermatt.

You'll find most paved Alpine roads, and even a few unpaved ones, described here. Most have been tested many times in both directions, and all have been rated by stars—two stars (★ ★) shouldn't be missed! All are discussed as part of a trip that includes a home base, hotels, and attractions. The trips and bases can be combined to fit almost any time frame and interest.

We used the following conventions when making the maps:

Map Legend

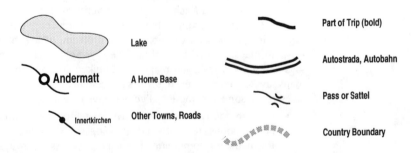

Lake

A Home Base

Andermatt

Innertkirchen   Other Towns, Roads

Part of Trip (bold)

Autostrada, Autobahn

Pass or Sattel

Country Boundary

Worth a Special Trip

Imagine the most exciting, the most beautiful, the best possible motorcycle trip.

There'd be roads, endless roads, climbing and sweeping through forests, past waterfalls and glaciers, bursting out into meadows, twisting past snow capped mountains.

There'd be green pastures with flowers and cowbells and farmhouses with flower boxes.

There'd be good food and shiny clean rest rooms, and maybe even motorcycle parking by the door.

And there'd be other motorcyclists, riding every kind of bike available on this planet.

Imagine this, and you've imagined the Alps. Motorcycle heaven with scenic overload.

There are other mountain ranges, but only in the Alps of Europe have people spent centuries building roads up into each high valley and in between each peak. Only in the Alps can you expect good food and drink at the top of the mountain.

In the Alps, good roads, good food, good hotels, good health standards, and a standard of living to equal or exceed any other all come together with exotic scenery and a general appreciation of motorcycling and driving.

Starting on the Mediterranean coast, the Alps arc across Europe, cutting off Italy's boot from the rest of the continent. Deep valleys cut into the mountains from all directions. Since ancient times, people have been trying to get from one valley

The endless supply of roads in the Alps includes lots of twisting and climbing. These hairpins on the east side of the Passo della Stelvio in Italy regularly entertain riders.

to the next. They hacked through gorges and hung roads on mountainsides, finally reaching a saddle, a pass, into the next valley. The ancients must have agonized over which pass to risk, how to carry supplies for a long journey, how to trade with the natives. Now, all those roads make a motorcycle paradise.

Just bring a credit card.

The south slopes of the Alps speak Italian, drink cappuccino, eat pasta and gelato at ristorantes and gelaterias, and drive Fiats and Moto Guzzis with skill on an amazing maze of mountain roads. They call a road over the mountain a "passo."

The westerly slopes speak French, drink wine, eat French fries and glace and French bread at restaurants with French doors, and drive Citroens and Renaults (say "wren oh") over some of the highest roads in the Alps. They call a road over the mountain a "col."

The north and east slopes of the Alps speak German, be they Austrian, Swiss, or Bavarian. They drink beer, eat Wiener-schnitzel (cutlet Viennese style) and Eis (say "ice") at Gasthofs. They drive BMWs and Mercedes very seriously on spectacular roads. They call a road over the mountain a "Pass."

There's something satisfying about a through road, one that goes up one side of the mountain and down the other side. In the Alps, such roads are known by the pass they traverse: Passo Sempione, or Grimsel Pass, or Col de l'Iseran. Each pass seems to have a unique personality.

At the core of all this is Switzerland. That's what we call it. German speakers who live there call it "Der Schweiz," French speakers call it "Suisse," Italian speakers who live there call it "Svizzera," and Swiss stamps call it "Helvetia." By any name, it's motorcycle heaven.

When the snow melts, Swiss put away their skis and get out their motorcycles. Motorcycling is so popular that German-speaking Swiss (Schweitzer Deutsch) have a special slang word for it: Toff (say "tough"). A Toffler, of course, is a biker. A

You'll see roads sweeping past glaciers and snow-capped mountains. These riders are on the south side of the Grimsel Pass in Switzerland with the Rhone Glacier in the background.

Gasthaus may have a sign, "Tofftreffpunkt," meaning a motorcycle meeting place. Tiny Switzerland even has its own motorcycle press, including a weekly magazine, *Moto Sport Schweiz*, published in both German and French.

Imagine you and your bike in the high Alps at Andermatt, in "der Schweiz." Every road in every direction is a great road. Select roads are marked here with a star. The creme de la creme, the absolute best roads, rate two. Some rate none, by Alpine standards, but those roads still must be among the best in the world. There isn't a bad one.

Near the top of the Furka Pass in Switzerland, the Finsteraarhorn dominates the western horizon. Under it, some of the best motorcycle riding in the world, the Grimsel Pass and the Furka Pass, meet down in the valley called Goms.

Good Stuff to Know

Of Shower Curtains, Window Screens, Sealing Wax, and Hair Dryers

Okay, if the Alps are so great, how come:
1. There aren't any window screens?
2. Or wash cloths?
3. The shower curtains are too small or non-existent?
4. My hair dryer fries?
5. Double beds aren't?
6. The feather bed is too hot and too small?
7. The steak is tough?
8. Water's rationed?
9. There aren't any laundromats?
10. There's that extra appliance in the bathroom?
11. They can't count?

1. It's true. The Alps are full of cows and all. They tinkle their bells and so forth everywhere. And there are no window screens in the Alps. Mechanically, there isn't a double-hung window in the Alps. All windows are on hinges, so screens aren't handy, and so the finest establishment may have flies. Almost all hotel rooms have a sheer curtain that can serve as a screen at night.

2. In the Alps, only branches of American hotel chains have wash cloths. Others may have a tray of toiletries, needle and thread, a razor, and an assortment of towels of all sizes, but no wash cloths. If a wash cloth is important, bring it from the New World.

3. For some reason, you're expected to sit down in the tub to shower with a hand-held shower on a flexible hose. So, why would you need a shower curtain? Some suggest that you are expected to wash before you shower. Maybe because Americans have flooded too many bathrooms, shower curtains are gaining a foothold in the Alps.

4. American appliances will not fit European plugs, voltage, or cycles. European plugs are round, and the prongs are too. Adapters are available, but their use usually burns up the appliance and trips the circuit breaker, leaving everybody unshaven, undried, and in the dark. Some electric razors will switch to 220, and will work with an adapter. Some hotels have outlets in the bath good for 110 SHAVERS ONLY. They will not

work with hair dryers. Hair dryers of modest price are available in Europe. Better to buy one there if it's absolutely needed. But they take up so much room! To save them and us the hassle, many hotels now have built-in hair dryers.

5. Almost all double beds are two singles pushed together. Sometimes, expressing a desire for a *grand lit* (a big bed, say "grahn lee"), or a "matrimonial bed," will help.

6. Everywhere that the Alps speak German—in Germany, Austria, north and west Switzerland, and the Sud Tirol part of Italy—beds have featherbeds. A featherbed is like a giant pillow, or maybe a fat comforter. It rests in a big hump on the bed, which otherwise is more or less similar to a bed anywhere. That means there's a sheet on the mattress, but no blankets, no cover sheet, and no bedspread. Just a luxurious featherbed stuffed inside a washable cover. Featherbeds vary in size and quilting. Without quilting, all the feathers may end up in one spot. Hardly ever will the thing cover the shoulders and feet at the same time. Some, in frustration, have been known to take the cover off the featherbed and crawl inside the cover. Better to curl up with the featherbed. It can be wonderful. If hot, leave a leg out, or more.

7. Steak is not an Alpine specialty. The hills are alive with music . . . it's cow bells. *Cow* bells. Not bull bells or steer bells. Boy cows become veal. The Alps have wonderful veal in all kinds of creative ways. But steak is very likely a mature cow.

8. Drinking tap water is very American. It's not customary in Europe. There's absolutely nothing wrong with drinking tap water in the Alps. It is always safe. But Europeans don't think it's a nice thing to do in public. Most hotel operators know that Americans have the uncouth habit of drinking water, even with meals, and they probably will make a modest carafe available upon request, but don't be surprised if the cook objects. It's reassuring to note that in the interest of safe driving, even the French have cut wine consumption dramatically in recent years, and Oktoberfest tents in Munchen are required to have alcohol-free drinks available. If it becomes an issue, get mineral water, with or without "gas." Some presumptuous hotels with stocked refrigerators in the room may have a little sign in the bathroom advising against drinking the tap water. It's a ruse.

9. There are hardly any self-laundries in Europe. For whatever reason, entrepreneurs don't deem them worthy. Be prepared to hand-wash whatever needs washing. Detergent works better than soap. Finer hotels will have pricey laundry service.

10. Hotel baths in Italy and France very often have bidets. They're for washing what's hard to wash in a basin. And for rinsing socks.

11. In Europe, the ground floor of a building is just that, the ground, the earth, terra firma. So the next floor up must be the

first floor. And what Americans would call the third floor is clearly labeled "2," etc.

Rest Stops

A roadside Gasthaus, hotel, or restaurant is a logical rest stop in the Alps. It's diplomatic to order something from the bar before using the facilities. Coffee, tea, and hot chocolate come from the bar in Europe, and each is made one cup at a time. No refills. In the home of Swiss chocolate, hot chocolate is a cup of hot milk and a package of powder. (The real thing is in Italy.) A hot fudge sundae is always good in Switzerland and is called a Coupe Danemark. In Switzerland, Sinalco is a carbonated grapefruit drink, and Rivella is like ginger ale. If you like the fizz, stop the waiter before the drink is dumped in a glass. There's always beer and wine, though most Euro restaurants feature only one local brew and few bars have hard liquor. Since the waiter will be charged for your order, pay and tip the waiter directly. In the Swiss countryside, the only currency is the Swiss Franc (a credit card slip signed in Swiss Francs will come home in dollars). If the bill is hand-written, remember that a European numeral "1" looks like an American "7," while Euro sevens have a horizontal line through them, and Europeans use a comma where Americans use a decimal point.

Spezi (say "SPAY zee") is a cola drink available in Bavaria and Austria. Soft drinks are a little less varied in France and Italy, so mineral water may be a safe bet.

Cold drinks hardly ever have ice. Ice cubes (*Eiswurfel* in German) are a rarity.

When

When is the best time to ride the Alps? Spring? Summer? Fall? The best time is as soon as possible, of course.

Late spring, May, and June, are spectacular. Eighteen hours of daylight illuminate meadows carpeted with new yellow and blue flowers. Flower boxes have new geraniums. High mountains, still snow capped, are awesome backdrops to larch trees, just showing new green needles. Gorges are gorged with white water. Temperatures are moderate, yet the high passes cut through deep canyons of snow. Even the southernmost reaches of the Alps should be temperate. The only problem is that some passes may still be snowed in. Any pass needed for access or commerce will be open, but those just for playing on, the more remote ones, may be awaiting sun and snow plows.

Come summer, all the passes open, and the south warms up. Seldom are the Alps really hot by American standards, but Italy and the south of France can be. August is vacation time in Europe, so major areas can be peopled, and prices may reflect "high season." Flower boxes are masses of pink, red, purple, and yellow. Steep mountain meadows are being mowed and raked by whole families. Cow bells tinkle until dark.

Fall can turn the meadows pink. Mountain ash trees are loaded with orange berries. Near the tree line, larch needles are turning yellow. Last winter's deep snows are long gone and the mountains show rocky faces. Streams are drier. Days are shorter. Most of the tourists go home. Sometimes a passing weather front can dust the mountains with new snow, perfectly etching each formation and crevice.

Some claim that there is less rain in the fall but any season in the Alps is a good season.

What to Wear

Europeans *expect* motorcyclists to wear leathers. A motorcyclist in full leathers will be welcome anywhere in the Alps.

Ideally, wear full leathers as the primary article of attire with only underwear, and maybe a turtleneck, under them.

A rain suit should go on easily over the leathers. The simplest is a hip-length jacket over elastic-waisted pants. (The jacket goes on first, so you don't get soaked pulling on the pants and so either top or bottom can be entered easily for keys or passport or whatever, without removing the other part.) One-piece rain suits work fine at keeping water out, but they sometimes are hard to get into and out of, especially dancing on the edge of the traveled lane, or in a small WC (water closet; toilet). Soleless, snap-on rain booties are effective and easy to use. Most rain boots are very hard to get on, and won't last if walked in. Remember, the boots go under the pants. Stores selling safety equipment have cheap and effective rain gloves to wear *over* leather gloves.

For cold, there should be a jacket to wear *over*, not under, the leathers. American softies have been known to enjoy an electric vest.

Even though spring days are warm and long, last winter's snows are still deep in the high country, especially in hairpins. Here, on Nufenen Pass, a snowblowing plow has opened the road.

Leathers can be wiped off and debugged at the end of the day, and underwear washed in the basin if necessary, but jeans draped over the flower boxes on the balcony probably won't dry overnight.

Sport clothing, maybe just a colorful warmup suit, will last a long time between washings if it's worn only a couple of hours in the evening.

Two-Night Stands: A Home Base

When you're reading a tour brochure at home, it does seem exciting to actually contemplate 12 exotic hotels in two weeks. But that takes a lot of packing and unpacking and hotel adjustment to move lineally along the road. Instead, how about establishing a base camp in an interesting smaller town like Andermatt? That means at least a couple of days of baggage-free riding; convenient, almost familiar, stores and shops; and a familiar home base at the end of a great riding day.

Gas and Oil and Service and Tires

Some Alpine roads seem otherworldly, like a wild moonscape. But the Alps are not Siberia, or even Alaska. Even the most remote mountain pass is just a few kilometers from civilization; Europe is a well-motorcycled population. There are services and probably motorcyclists in every town and village, down at the bottom of the pass. And if you're at the top of the pass, everything is downhill.

Gas stations are plentiful, but not on mountain tops. Since they weren't in any medieval town plan, most are located outside the historical old parts of cities and towns and near the edge of smaller communities. Everything about a gas station looks familiar, with pumps and islands—everything, that is, but the price, which will be three or four times the U.S. price. Both gas and oil are sold by the liter. Leaded gas is being phased out, but both leaded and unleaded have higher octane than is available in the U.S.

In many smaller localities, stations close for a two-hour lunch at noon. Some stations announce that they are open (little signs, "aperto," or "ouvert"), but only for drivers paying via automated credit card or cash machines.

Air is most likely available from a portable canister with a dial on the top. The canister hangs from a filler valve. Usually, the dial has pressure readings in both metric and pounds. The metric unit of pressure is kilograms per square centimeter (usually called "bar"). One pound per square inch equals 0.07 bar; 33 pounds per square inch is about 2.33 bar. Finicky tire adjusters might want to carry a pocket gauge.

Most communities of any size have at least one motorcycle shop. At many the staff may appear busy even if they are not, so scheduling service in advance is wise. Store hours and days vary. Most depend on overnight delivery of parts from some central warehouse. Best way to find a shop is in the phone book, the yellow pages, or in motorcycle magazines, or by asking another biker. Smiles and pointing always help in an emergency. Pointing at a worn tire or a brake pad or a headlamp, etc., will register with most riders, dealers, and mechanics. They've probably been on the wrong side of a language barrier themselves.

An American on the Italian island of Sardinia once cracked a wheel hub on a BMW ST, not a very common bike. Calling around and using all possible translators, he learned about an overnight ferry from Sardinia to Genova on the mainland. The broken BMW was to take the ferry to Genova. Meantime, the BMW dealer in Genova would order a new hub from the BMW importer in Verona, Italy, and the hub would get to Genova overnight, too. The bike made it on the ferry. Other bikers on the ferry helped find the dealer in Genova. The hub arrived from Verona as scheduled, delivered by a 3-wheeled Lambretta truck. The wheel was laced and the American was off and running for the Alps that day.

Accelerating and braking and leaning on twisty roads all day long may wear tires faster than normal. Nothing spoils the enjoyment of a good road like worrying about a tire. Many motorcycle shops do not sell motorcycle tires. Tire stores do and usually they will mount them for you. A motorcycle dealer may send out to the tire store for the needed tire and then mount it for you. Dealers will want to follow the law, which requires them to mount only matching, factory approved tires.

Calling America

Most U.S. telephone companies have a "USA Direct" service. In each foreign country there's a toll-free number to call and the U.S. operator answers. It's cheaper and it's easier than dialing direct. The charge goes on your credit card or phone bill. Carry the numbers for the company you use. A call from a hotel room using the USA Direct number should not record on a hotel's billing machines.

	AT&T	MCI	Sprint
Austria	022-903-011	022-903-012	022-903-014
France	19 [tone] 0011	19 [tone] 0019	190-087
Germany	0130-0010	0130-0012 (western only)	0130-0013 (western only)
Italy	172-1011	172-1022	172-1877 (public phones may require coin)
Liechtenstein	155-0011	155-0222	155-9777
Switzerland	155-0011	155-0222	155-9777 (public phones require coin or card)

Calling Europe

It's really cheap during low-rate hours. Mid-day in Europe is early morning in the U.S.—the cheapest time to call.

In the U.S. dial 011 to get the international circuit. Then dial the country code (41 for Switzerland, 39 for Italy, or 33 for France), then the area code (for example, the area code for Andermatt is 44) and the desired number.

Most Europeans list their phone with the area code first, and a zero in front of the area code. The zero is like a "1" in America. Use it the same way. Dial it first to call out of the local area from within the same country. It isn't necessary if the call is originating inside that area, or if calling from another country. When calling to a European country from America or any other country, just use the country code and the area code. No zero.

Of course, the answering party may speak very fast in German or Italian or some other language. If uncertain, ask for "English, please."

Except for big city hotels, hotel staffs in Europe go to bed, so there may not be any answer in the middle of the night.

Demi-Pension

Almost every hotel in Europe will make a special price for "demi-pension," half pension, which is room, dinner, and breakfast. Full pension includes lunch. Quite often demi-pension is a good deal, and maybe a necessity in remote locations. Sometimes there will be a choice available at dinner, sometimes not. Most of the time, breakfast is a buffet with a variety of wonderful fresh breads (no breakfast until the bakery has delivered), cold cuts, cheese, and possibly nowadays, juice and fruit, but hardly ever eggs.

Bread and rolls are delicious in Europe and are served at all meals. Most Europeans visiting the U.S. say what they miss most is good bread. Good beer is a distant second.

In Europe, butter comes only at breakfast. Demi-pension prices are per-person.

Cash Money

Border crossings are a regular fact of riding in the Alps. Alpine riders go back and forth across national borders often. On one side of the fence they may have good cappuccino, and on the other, not. But on either side it's advantageous, and possibly necessary, to pay in local currency. Credit card transactions are always in local currency, with the bank changing to dollars for billing. Austria is the only country where even waiters are prepared to deal in foreign currencies, although usually to their own advantage. So several purses or wallets are handy to keep each country's money readily available.

Only major border crossings have currency exchanges. "Change" is often the identifying sign, although the German word is "Wechseln" and the Italian, "cambio." Banks and train stations also usually have exchanges. In rural train stations, the ticket seller does the changing. Sometimes it's necessary to go to one teller to make the exchange, and then to a cashier to get the money.

In Europe, the custom is to wait in line to the right of the person being served. Waiting behind the person being served may lead the locals to assume that the ugly American is trying to crash the line (and vice versa). Watch what others are doing.

Some Italian crossings have auto club offices marked "ACI" (Auto Club Italia) that will change money. Hotels will change money, but often at a less desirable rate. All will charge a fee. Most of the time it's just as well to keep reserve funds in dollars. It's often cheaper to exchange traveler's checks than cash.

It's never advantageous to change twice, for example get Italian lira for dollars in Switzerland. There'll be a fee for changing to Swiss francs, then another for changing to lira.

But whatever the fee, it's nice to have a little "real," that is local, money in your pocket.

Passports and Stuff

There are two checks at border crossings, including airports: a passport check, to identify the person; and a customs check to identify the "stuff." At most small border crossings in the Alps, the same official checks both. But there will still be two checks. The country you're leaving will check you out. Then, after you've crossed the border, the country you're entering will check you in. The two checks may be some kilometers apart. Usually, the customs folk are more interested in what natives may be bringing back than what visitors are carrying. With the coming of European union, there is less hassle, even about insurance, since it's assumed that everyone must be legal. Should a border guard note a non-European license plate, he'll

Alpine riders cross international borders often. Here, a group leaves Italy at the Splugen Pass. Usually the border guard wants to see a passport only when it's buried deep under several layers of clothing.

very likely decide to check insurance papers. On some remote unstaffed crossings, a little sign may say something to the effect of, "If you have something to declare, stop in the next town."

Always remember, you and your bike are passing through, not entering to stay. Americans don't need visas, but riders must have their valid driver's licenses, and preferably an international one (available from auto clubs in the U.S.) as well as a passport.

A thin wallet on a string around your neck is handy for passports and official papers. Inexpensive ones are sold in hiking and camping and bicycle shops in America and motorcycle shops in Europe. A passport in your luggage is almost useless.

So What Are We Going to Call It?

We call it Germany. Italians call it Germania. French call it Allemagne. But the Germans call it Deutschland.

We call it Lake Geneva. Germans call it Genfersee. The folks who live there call it Lac Leman.

We call it Venice. So do the French. The Germans call it Venedig. Italians call it Venezia.

Most of us call it the Matterhorn. But half of it is in Italy where it's Monte Cervino.

Most signs will be local. So will most maps. So, it's the intent here to use local names. The exception: herein it's Germany and Austria and Italy, not Deutschland and Osterreich and Italia, even though that's what local signs will say (except in Italy, where signs pointing to Austria will say Austria). The international code is used everywhere in the Alps, and here: (D) is Deutschland, Germany. (A) is Osterreich, Austria. (CH) is Der Schweiz, Switzerland. (I) is Italia, Italy. (F) is France. (FL) is Liechtenstein. Accordingly, Swiss bikes and cars are identified by a "CH" sticker, presumably for "Confederation Helvetia."

Germans put two dots over some vowels. They are called "umlauts" and are supposed to help in pronunciation. For example, there are supposed to be two dots over the u in Zürich and also over the u in München. Some texts leave out the dots but add an e, so it's Zuerich and Muenchen. That all seems confusing. Here, there will be no dots and no e's.

Sometimes Germans use a letter that looks something like a capital B (β) instead of a double s at the end of a word like "pass." Here, it will always be double s.

And, Germans have the habit of tacking modifiers onto a word without spacing, so that a menu item might read "Grandmothersrecipeforsteakontoast," or a highway sign, "Oberalppass." Here it will be "grandmothers recipe for steak on toast," and "Oberalp Pass."

Besonder Uberwachung und Versicherung und Umleitung, or, "Special watching and insurance and detour"

Some German words don't slide easily from the English speaker's tongue. The French and Italian equivalents almost make good sense. But a couple of German words like those above are not in most handy "where is a good restaurant?" guides.

Besonder Uberwachung is on signs around Austria under a picture of a motorcycle. Motorcyclists will be especially watched! Other signs at Austrian borders advise that Austrian police use radar "in the whole land." Radar traps exist, especially in Austria. Typically, there is an unmarked radar in some area with a speed limit, like a village of a couple of houses, and the police wait farther along the road at the edge of the village and pull hapless drivers or riders over, waving them in with a red "ping pong" paddle. Friendly as Austrians are, their police will extract fines on the spot in cash for speeding. Most police in Europe do the same.

Recently, Austria has put signs along the road that show a motorcyclist with an angel above, and words to the effect of, "give your guardian angel a chance." Switzerland has had signs picturing a rider with the words "look out." Most auto drivers assume it is the rider who is supposed to look out!

Helmets are mandatory in the Alps. Some countries require headlights at all times.

The international sign showing a motorcycle (usually ancient) in profile in a red circle means "motorcycles forbidden." The key is the little white sign underneath it, reading something like "between 2230 and 0600." There's often a second white sign that reads something like "except for bikes with business in the area."

Germany has a lot of low speed limit signs, even on Autobahns. The key is the little white sign underneath that says *Bei Nasse,* "when wet."

Versicherung, insurance, is mandatory. Proof of liability insurance is required before a vehicle license plate is issued in Europe. And it's fairly expensive, like thousands of dollars a year. Many motorcyclists turn in their license plate for the winter to save on insurance costs. Rental bikes should already be insured. Insurance should be included with any bike purchased in Europe. Bikes brought from America must have proof of European insurance before they're allowed out of customs.

Americans living or stationed in Europe can get motorcycle insurance like car insurance. But few U.S. carriers will or can sell it to Americans traveling for pleasure. European insurance companies complain of bad luck with American bikers. Proof of insurance is a green piece of paper called a green card. That's what police and border agents will want to see.

European liability (and only liability) insurance can be purchased for U.S.-registered bikes from these two sources in New York City:

- Overseas International Brokerage, 212-541-5860
- American International Underwriters, 212-770-8912

The American Automobile Association (national headquarters in Heathrow, Florida) offers a variety of insurance coverage for American tourists, including collision, theft, and medical: 800-222-4599; FAX 407-444-8567.

Switzerland has a special organization for medical evacuation. It uses helicopters and jets to pick up sick or injured people and return them to Swiss hospitals. By special arrangements, it can operate from the roadside in nearby countries, flying directly to Switzerland. It is designed to serve Swiss nationals, but it also can serve members who pay a modest annual membership fee of about $20 (always listed in Swiss francs, but they accept checks in dollars). It communicates almost exclusively in German and its name is a twister, *Rettungsflugwacht,* which roughly translates to "emergency flight service." It's called REGA for short. It's designed to get Swiss nationals home from the Andes or Kansas as well as the Alps, a part of the service that Americans probably aren't interested in. Address: REGA, Mainaustrasse 21, CH-800B Zurich, Switzerland. Phone: 01/385 8585.

Fun mountain roads are labor-intensive, and the labor usually can only be done in summer, when the roads are open and the ice is gone. Detours are a possibility, labeled "deviazione" in Italian and *Umleitung* in German. Sometimes a portable traffic signal allows traffic past the repair area one way at a time. It's common, though not legal, for bikes to go to the front of any line waiting for the green, with the obligation, of course, to take off fast when the light turns green so as not to delay others. A tardy response to the green will elicit some angry responses from other drivers with whom the road may have to be shared. On popular bike roads, the light may collect quite an array of motorcycles, and the green light is almost like the start of a race. It does make sense to get ahead of any trucks or buses.

Where Are They From?

Everybody plays the game of guessing where their fellow travelers are from. License plates help. Cognoscenti can tell which town a long French license plate comes from. Some insist that shoes and socks (or lack thereof) are telltale. Chances are that any American will be identified as such without saying a word, especially while eating. Only right-handed Americans hold a fork in the right hand. Only Americans ever put the other hand below the table. Right-handed Europeans hold the knife in the right hand and the fork in the left. So, it's hard for an American to hide. In Europe, there have been plenty of wars, with bombings and occupations and refugees and invasions, unpleasant invasions of tourists as well as soldiers. Everybody has had plenty of opportunity to develop prejudices as well as preferences. In the long run, American is one of the better things to be.

Europeans all know of U.S. speed limits, and presume no American can go over 55. Keeping up with local traffic can be helpful as well as entertaining. British and Dutch drivers usually stand out because they have orange license plates. Both are usually very cautious in the mountains—the Dutch because they have no mountains to practice on, and the poor British because the driver is seated on the wrong side of the car and can't see the road ahead. At least both speak good English. (How far can you go speaking Dutch?) Locals are almost always more aggressive drivers than visitors.

A couple of American customs need modification in the Alps. The forefinger raised when ordering means two, like "two beers" (it is the second finger). The thumb raised means one beer. And the thumb and forefinger touching, the okay sign in America, is not okay in the Alps. The middle finger? Let's hope it's three beers.

News

In America, many newsstands carry *The European,* a British paper of continental news. It is a good way to find out what's happening in the Alps, including weather, road conditions, and status of Alpine passes. In Europe, most newsstands have two American newspapers, the *Herald Tribune,* and *USA Today,* both printed in Europe.

Road Signs and Drivers

Alpine signs almost always point toward towns and passes.

Road signs usually emphasize pass names, along with some of the possible towns down the road, but not every possible town. Furka Oberalp is a railroad that carries vehicles. (Andermatt)

Route numbers are obscure. It's best to know which town you're going to.

City limit signs are automatic speed limit signs, and villages and towns are where speed laws are usually enforced. Conversely, the end of a city, the city sign with a slash through it, means "resume highway speed."

Direction arrows often point *at* the road, which may not necessarily be the direction of travel. For instance, an arrow on the left side of the road pointing right most likely does not mean turn right. It means that "this is the road."

Schematic signs of anticipated intersections don't necessarily mean "now." There are often signs diagramming how roads will intersect in the next town.

You usually can't go around the block. If you miss a corner in a city, there probably will be another sign to the destination. If all else fails in a city or town, head back for the middle and start again. All towns have signs to the middle: "Stadtmitte," in German, "centro," in Italian. French have a wonderful sign: "toutes directions," meaning "you can get anywhere going this way." The yellow diamond sign used in Europe means "this road has the right of way over all entering or cross traffic." A slash mark through any sign means the end of it, whatever it was. A slash across a white circle means the end of whatever was being regulated, like the speed.

European drivers are usually very good and alert. Driver's licenses are expensive and hard to get, and motorcycle licenses almost always require expensive schools and long periods of probation. European drivers will expect you to be competent and alert, too. If you are, they will usually accommodate you. Just remember, they consider the road to be a commodity in short supply. Anybody on it should be using it. Don't block the road. Some rules of the road and right of way are different than in America, and it sure helps to know them (for example, no turn on red in Europe, and no passing on the right on a freeway).

Skid marks on mountain roads are evidence that not all drivers have been perfect. Sometimes the marks head in unsatisfactory directions.

Time to ride.

Around
Andermatt

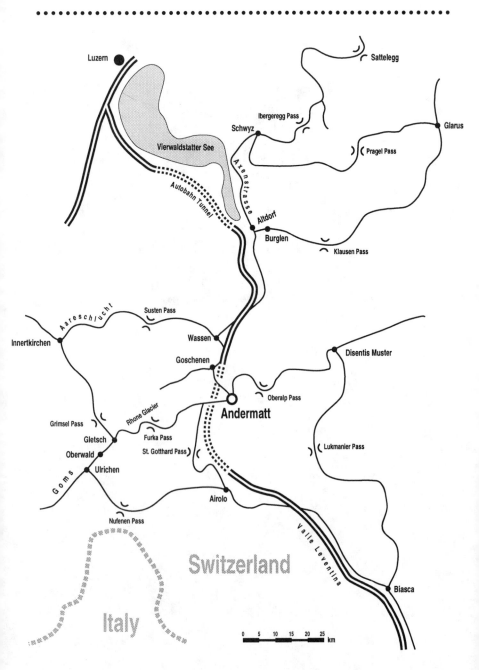

Andermatt

Draw a straight line across the Alps from Milano, Italy, to Zurich, Switzerland. Right in the middle of that line, in the very middle of the Alps, is Andermatt, Switzerland.

Imagine you and your bike in Andermatt, in the mountain canton called Uri. There are four major Alpine trips over some of the highest passes through some of the most spectacular country in the Alps starting right in Andermatt. Uncluttered by cities, these trips are good in any order, in any direction.

The village of Andermatt, at 1450 meters, is almost as high as Zermatt. Zermatt has the Matterhorn and hoards of tourists. But Zermatt doesn't have any roads. Andermatt does.

For centuries, Andermatt was the crossroads of the Alps: Italy to the south, France to the west, Germany to the north, Austria to the east. Now, thanks to the longest highway tunnel in the world, tour buses and trucks, everybody with fear of heights, and anyone with urgent business, all go through the mountain instead of through Andermatt. Andermatt is for Alpinists and motorcyclists. That's what this book is about—where the crowds don't go but motorcycles do.

Park by the cafe of the **Hotel Monopol-Metropol** in Andermatt. You're on the inside corner of one of the best sweeper roads in the world, the Oberalp Pass. It starts right there at the hotel. The first sweep goes around the hotel. The road continues, arc after arc of smooth asphalt, never straightening out, up the face of the mountain.

Andermatt has gas stations, restaurants, hotels, and shops, all along a cobblestone street with granite slabs for wagon wheel tracks. Most everything about the gas station will seem familiar—except the price.

In mid-summer, it's light until after 10 p.m., and bikes come from the great cities in the valleys to drive the Oberalp in the evening. The pass is worth several passes. (Mind the decreasing radius in the tunnel, coming down.)

Looking down from the sweepers of the Oberalp, you can see Andermatt huddled in a corner of its mountain-ringed valley, some modern buildings, some shingled chalets, some log buildings, with a Baroque church tower above all. The cobblestone main street has smooth granite slabs for wagon wheels. The street looks ancient, but was brand new in the 1980's.

A hypotenuse bypass leads across the valley from the granite Kaserne (military base) toward the St. Gotthard Pass. A cable car goes from the west side of the village up on Gemsstock Mountain, 1500 meters above the town. The cog railway weaving around the Oberalp road leads down to a train station in Andermatt, where it meets two other cog lines. This is the land of the Glacier Express train between Zermatt and St. Moritz.

Andermatt has restaurants, gas stations, banks, shops, and the Post, Switzerland's post office, telephone exchange, and bus station. You can dial anywhere in the world from the Post and pay when the call is completed. Just remember that the east coast is six hours behind the Alps, and the west coast nine hours. So 6 p.m. in Andermatt is noon in New York and 9 a.m. in California. All the Alps have daylight savings time. They just start and end on different dates than ours in the U.S. and even than other countries in Europe.

The Post is where all those yellow buses park, the public buses that deliberately motor into every cranny of Switzerland, sometimes towing a baggage trailer and tootling their three-note horn. The horn is supposed to send all other traffic scrambling to get out of the way. Most importantly, the Post sells freeway stickers that all vehicles must have to drive on a Swiss freeway, including many tunnels and many two-lane roads that have limited access. There are no toll roads in Switzerland.

From the Hotel Monopol Metropol in Andermatt, watch the parade. From all over the world, riders come to the sweepers of the Oberalp Pass. The first sweep goes right around the hotel.

Andermatt's travel bureau is: **Verkehrsburo,** CH-6490 Andermatt, Switzerland. (In Euro addresses the ZIP comes before the town. In this instance, 6490 is the ZIP, CH is the code for Switzerland.) Phone 044/ 6 74 54; FAX 044/ 6 81 85.

A sampling of the many hotels in Andermatt includes:

The **Hotel Monopol-Metropol,** located on the corner where the Oberalp begins, is a building with an international flavor and a kitchen that blends Swiss and French cooking. CH-6490 Andermatt; phone 044/ 675 75; FAX 044/ 679 23.

The **Drei Konige Hotel** (three kings, as in "We Three Kings of Orient Are") is located in the crook of the cobblestone street through Andermatt, right beside a rushing mountain torrent. It's traditional Swiss. CH-6490 Andermatt; phone 044/ 672 03; FAX 044/ 676 66.

The **Sporthotel Sonne** (sun) is a multi-story log building in the center of the village, with a door that opens directly onto the cobblestone street. It's much more modern than it looks, with a cozy dining room and a garage for motorcycles. CH-6490 Andermatt; phone 044/ 672 26.

In any language, Swiss money is called a Franc. Traveler's checks and money can be changed at a bank or at any Swiss train station.

German is the working language of Andermatt, but most locals can speak some English. The waitress may be a Norwegian who spent her last holiday in San Francisco, while the clerk in the sport shop very likely can discuss slopes at Aspen.

Besides the Oberalp Pass heading east, three roads lead out of Andermatt. West across the valley beyond Andermatt, the Furka Pass snakes up the mountain. Compared to the Oberalp, it's narrow and tight and irregular. Working up the mountain south is the St. Gotthard Pass. To the north an unbelievable road squeezes through a gorge called the Schollenen, made by the Reuss River.

Keep the bike on that granite slab! On the crook of the cobblestone street through Andermatt, right where the street crosses over a mountain stream, is the Hotel Drei Konige. Behind are sweepers of the Oberalp Pass.

Trip 1 Furka, Grimsel, Susten

Distance   *About 120 kilometers from Andermatt*

Terrain   *Steep twisting climbs into glacier worlds, three steep twisting descents, plus the narrow Schollenen gorge, mostly modern highway. Some tunnels.*

Highlights   *Rhone Glacier, Aareschlucht water storm, favorite motorcycle cafes, Sherlock Holmes site, Devil's Bridge and stone, Autobahn tunnel entrance, Furka Pass (2431 meters), Grimsel Pass (2165 meters), and Susten Pass (2224 meters), the Schollenen Gorge*

At 2431 meters, the Furka Pass is one of the higher roads in the Alps. Just a few kilometers from Andermatt, up among glacial peaks and rushing water, it's easy to feel civilization is very far away. Climbing west from Andermatt, the snaking Furka is too narrow for a center line. Larger vehicles need more than half of the road. Granite pylons mark the edge of the pavement and the beginning of open space. Motorcycles rule because they're about the only vehicles that can pass. Still, no vehicle gets more of the road than it needs, so a slow bike may get passed very close aboard.

At the top there's what could pass for an unpaved parking lot on the south side. From it, a graded road heads up around the adjoining mountain, and from the graded road, a magnificent view of the **Rhone Valley,** called the Goms, and the mass of the **Rhone Glacier,** and the cantilevered hairpins of the Furka, and the zig zags of the Grimsel Pass climbing the far mountain, and the lake at the top of the Grimsel, and the peaks beyond, and . . .

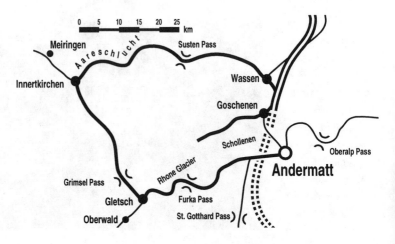

The westerly side of the Furka is mostly new alignment. Then at one hairpin, you're face to face with the Rhone Glacier. Drive right up to the base of the ice, source of the Rhone River. Water melting from this glacier runs to the Mediterranean at Marseille, France. (Back at Andermatt, all the water was running to the Rhine and the North Sea.) At the glacier there's a parking lot terraced on the edge of the mountain, with an outdoor cafe that's popular with bikers. Restrooms are down under the parking lot. A tunnel carved into the glacier permits a walk into the blue world inside.

It's only 31 kilometers from Andermatt, across the Furka Pass and past the Rhone Glacier, down to Gletsch, where the Grimsel Pass road intersects and heads up and north. Gletsch is just a couple of stone buildings at the tree line.

The traversing road up the Grimsel leads to hairpins supported by walls of massive stones and offering great views of the Rhone Glacier.

Several restaurants around the lake at the top of the Grimsel are popular with motorcyclists. The one farthest north, **Hotel Alpenrosli,** has parking by the door for motorcycles only. A big parking lot across the road is sometimes full of bikes. The outdoor terrace is popular on sunny days.

It's 37 kilometers north from Gletsch across the Grimsel, past hydroelectric plants and through forests and meadows to Innertkirchen, where the Susten Pass road heads east. This is countryside known in song and story as the Berner (Bernese) Oberland, canton Bern, the valley of the Aare River. Just a few kilometers below Innertkirchen, the Aare goes through a very narrow gorge called a *Schlucht,* as in *Aareschlucht.* It's a spectacular display of enormous volumes of frothing water. There's a parking lot on a hairpin where a wooden catwalk leads into the water storm.

Just below the Schlucht is the base of the **Reichenbach**

Bikes charge a hairpin on the Furka Pass that's been modernized by extending it on stilts over space. That's more of the Furka continuing on the left down to the the village of Gletsch. The Grimsel climbs the far slope.

Waterfall, the great cascade where Arthur Conan Doyle had Sherlock Holmes fall to his death in a fight with the villain Moriarty. A marker at the base of the falls says it happened on May 4, 1891. It must be so, because the monument was erected by "The Norwegian Explorers of Minnesota!" There's a statue of the great detective in the nearby village of **Meiringen.**

The climb up the Susten Pass from Innertkirchen goes from meadows back up to the land of glaciers. The parking lot at the top of the Susten Pass, surrounded by glaciers, is another favorite motorcycle gathering place. The restaurant has a view terrace from which there's free access to the restrooms below (Euro restrooms are usually marked "WC").

The road east is a tunnel. Sit on the terrace and try to identify the bikes coming from the east by their exhaust note magnified in the tunnel. Some of the road beyond the tunnel was taken out by an avalanche, and the replacement is one-lane, one-way-at-a-time in accordance with posted times. You're on your honor, using your own watch or clock. Often, bikes gather in significant numbers to start down at the appointed time.

It's 53 kilometers across the Susten Pass from Innertkirchen on the west to Wassen on the east. The final curves down into Wassen offer views of one of the major engineering feats of the Alps, the four-lane freeway in the gorge of the Reuss River. The gorge is so narrow and steep that the road is either on a bridge or in a tunnel. Here it's called an Autobahn, and it leads to the tunnel under Andermatt, the longest vehicle tunnel in the world.

It's only a couple of kilometers south, up the Schollenen from Wassen to Goschenen, where the freeway enters the long tunnel, and where the really steep part of the gorge begins. The main line of the railroad goes in a tunnel, too, leaving only a cog line to grind on up to Andermatt alongside the gorge road. (There's a fun dead-end road westerly from Goschenen to a high Alpine lake.)

The road snaking up the west side of the Susten Pass cuts through the mountain, while a mountain stream goes over it, and then becomes a waterfall.

By the freeway entrance to the long tunnel is a **giant rock** with the flag of canton Uri on it: gold, with a black bull's head with a ring in its nose and a red tongue hanging out. The big rock was moved aside at great expense during freeway construction because:

> Long ago, the villagers failed to get a bridge across the gorge. The devil offered to build it in exchange for the soul of the first to cross the bridge. But the villagers fooled the devil by sending a goat across the bridge first. Enraged, the devil hoisted the huge rock to smash the bridge, only to drop the rock when a villager made the sign of the cross.

The rock's still there to prove it. Pictures of the **Teufelbrucke (Devil's Bridge)** abound around Andermatt.

The climb up the gorge toward Andermatt goes right by the Devil's Bridge and another bridge of Roman origin. And there's a spot in the gorge that will be forever Russian. A turn-off near the Devil's Bridge leads down to an enormous carving in the mountainside with script in Cyrillic. Seems it commemorates a Russian army. Defeated by Napoleon on the plains, it retreated south and was trapped in the gorge.

A final short tunnel opens out onto the high Andermatt valley. The main road is the hypotenuse bearing right toward the St. Gotthard Pass. A mini interchange leads into the village, past the vast stone Kaserne, home to much of Switzerland's citizen army. In the village, soldiers patrol around and occasionally roar by in rubber-treaded tanks, or astride an army Condor motorcycle, assembled in Switzerland with a Ducati engine.

Remember the DB-1 Bimota that was on the cover of every bike magazine once? There it was, parked in Andermatt. Tiny, beautiful. Tracked down, the owner allowed as how it had indeed cost a bundle of Swiss Francs. "You could have bought a Harley for that!" The owner reached into a pocket and pulled out a card. He was a Harley dealer.

After a fun-filled ride up the hairpins and twisties of the Susten Pass, most bikers are ready to kick tires a minute and perhaps check the scene from the terrace of the restaurant. Bikes often pack the parking lot.

Trip 2 St. Gotthard, Nufenen, Furka

Distance	*About 110 kilometers from Andermatt*
Terrain	*Three steep twisting climbs and descents, mostly modern highways*
Highlights	*St. Gotthard Museum, a favorite motorcycle cafe, concrete-roofed sweepers, in and out of Italian-speaking, cappuccino land, St. Gotthard Pass (2108 meters), Nufenen Pass (Switzerland's highest at 2478 meters), Furka Pass (2431 meters)*

It's a good sweeping ride up the St. Gotthard to the top, where all of a sudden, it's no longer the St. Gotthard, but the San Gottardo. The south slopes of the Alps speak Italian, eat pasta, and drink cappuccino, even in Switzerland. The old-time hospice at the pass summit has been turned into a museum of the historic attempts to conquer the pass, including the history of the Devil's Bridge. Water here runs to the Po River in Italy, and thence to the Adriatic. A monument out front commemorates aviators' attempts to conquer the pass. Crossing the Alps in early planes was a major undertaking.

Behind the museum there's a short stretch of the old cobblestone road down to the south. It's very photogenic but not a lot of fun to ride. It's usually closed to through traffic.

A lot of the southern slope of the St. Gotthard is in kilometer-long, covered concrete sheds, to protect motorists from avalanche. The sheds are open on one side, and the road surface is good at highway speed.

The longest vehicle tunnel in the world, the one that enters the mountain as an Autobahn at Goschenen on the north side of Andermatt, comes out on the south slopes of the pass at

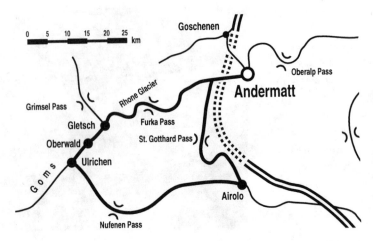

Airolo as an autostrada, having passed under all these good roads. By following the signs for Passo della Novena (that's what the Nufenen is called in Italian) it's possible to avoid getting involved in the tunnel traffic at Airolo. The Nufenen, a newly laid out road and one of the highest in Switzerland, climbs west out of Airolo.

Often photographed are the **three flags** flying at the top of the Nufenen, the Swiss flag flanked by those of the two cantons connected by the pass, Ticino and Wallis. Behind the flags, way across the Goms valley, are the peaks of the Berner Oberland, including the Jungfrau. The most prominent as viewed from the Nufenen is the Finsteraarhorn at 4274 meters.

The cafeteria at the top of the pass is popular with bikers, because the northerly descent, way down into the Goms at Ulrichen, is a wonderful piece of road: good pavement, steep, and full of predictable hairpins.

Ulrichen is down in meadowlands, so it's a real climb back up and east to Gletsch where the Furka and Grimsel meet. The road passes some military airstrips and the railroad loading ramps at **Oberwald,** where cars and motorcycles can be driven right onto the train for a tunnel ride under the Furka Pass back to Andermatt. Should you choose this method, just ride onto a flat car and take a seat in a passenger compartment. Switzerland claims to be planning a steam cog train using the old abandoned tracks over the pass.

The parking lot of the Rhone Glacier revealed a bunch of bikes, including a YB-1 Bimota. The rider turned out to be a dentist from Disentis, over the Oberalp from Andermatt. "Your English sure is good." "Oh, I teach part time at the University of Illinois!"

A monument out in front of the museum atop the St. Gotthard Pass commemorates early attempts to fly over the pass. The museum traces valiant efforts to conquer the pass, culminating in the present road of sweeping curves.

Trip 3   Oberalp, Lukmanier, St. Gotthard

Distance	*About 154 kilometers*
Terrain	*Three climbs and descents, plus a valley run*
Highlights	*Oberalp Pass (2044 meters) and the world's best sweepers, less-traveled Lukmanier Pass (1914 meters), St. Gotthard Pass (2108 meters), a taste of Romansch culture, deeper into Italian-speaking Switzerland*

Sweep up the Oberalp from Andermatt into canton Graubunden (sometimes called Grisons in English), where buildings are usually stucco with arches and deep set windows and stenciled decoration. The official language is Romansch. Nobody speaks it, but they print signs in it. The working language remains German.

Across the Oberalp, at a pretty good sized town called **Disentis-Muster,** the Lukmanier Pass road heads south. Disentis is famous for a big monastery church visible just above the town. To visit it, you have to park below on the main road and hike up. The interior is sort of Spanish baroque. To head for the Lukmanier, take a sharp right in the middle of the town down across the Vorderrhein River. The sign for the pass in Romansch

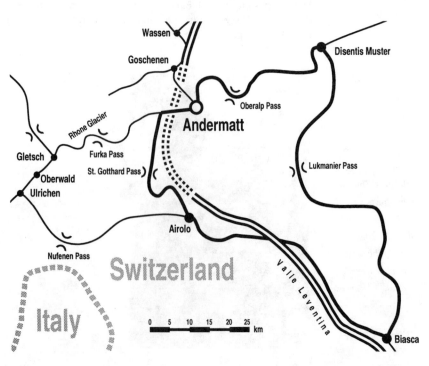

40

will be "Cuolm Lucmagn." As soon as you cross the pass, the signs will be in Italian, and the pass will be called Passo del Lucomagno. The pass road is modern all the way to Biasca, where it meets the St. Gotthard road. There's a functional restaurant at the top.

Biasca is in one of those major valleys that cut deep into the Alps, the Valle Leventina. It's the best route from the great cities of Italy to Zurich, via the long St. Gotthard tunnel. So a lot of traffic is heading for the St. Gotthard (called "San Gottardo" here), and since it's about 35 kilometers north, the autostrada may be the viable route to get there. Just be sure to exit the autostrada at Airolo, or you'll be treated to at least 20 minutes of tunnel behind a diesel-belching bus or truck, all the way to Goschenen.

On the climb up the St. Gotthard from Airolo there are a couple of tight sweepers on stilts out over the valley, with big metal expansion joints that are slippery when wet. A turnout has a little restaurant with a fine view of the can-of-worms interchange squeezed into the valley down in Airolo where the autostrada, the tunnel, the Nufenen Pass and the St. Gotthard Pass roads all meet.

A Kawasaki pulled into the restaurant at the top of the Lukmanier once. The rider was all in white—white leathers, white boots, white gloves. He allowed he worked for Swissair. "How do you keep it white?" "Oh, that's my wife's job!"

On long summer evenings, bikers come from the great cities of Europe, not to mention the rest of the world, just to ride the sweepers of the Oberalp Pass above Andermatt.

Trip 4   Klausen, Pragel, the 'eggs'

Distance	*About 200 kilometers from Andermatt*
Terrain	*Tight climbs and descents on narrow, less-traveled roads*
Highlights	*William Tell country, a historic highway on lakeshore, Klausen Pass (1948 meters), Switzerland's little-known Pragel Pass (1550 meters), Ibergeregg (1406 meters), Sattelegg (1190 meters)*

★ ★

Dash north down the Schollenen Gorge and hop on that Alpine masterpiece, the Autobahn, down toward Luzern. In a couple of minutes, you'll be in Altdorf, almost at sea level, at least the level of Lake Luzern. Klausen Pass climbs east from Altdorf.

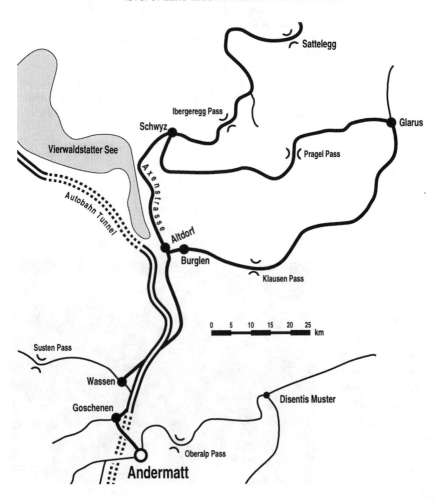

Altdorf is famous as the home of William Tell and there's a monument and statue of him and his son in the center of the town. Tell was not just a good marksman, but a symbol of Swiss independence. The guy who had him shoot the apple off his son's head back in the middle ages was the evil count, an outsider. It seems that four of the Swiss forest cantons around Lake Luzern decided they'd like to be independent. The count was against it. Tell was for it. The evil count dreamed up the ultimate punishment for a father—the life of his son. He was sure that the son would flinch or Tell would miss, or both. We all know that the son didn't and Tell didn't.

The lake that we call **Lake Luzern** the Swiss call by the tongue twister Vierwaldstatter See (four forest state sea) after the four cantons of Tell's day. And we call the country "Switzerland" after Schwyz, one of the four forest cantons.

Climbing out of Altdorf on the Klausen, the next village is Burglen, Tell's home, where there's a smaller statue of Tell.

About halfway up the Klausen from Altdorf, on the inside of a 180, there's an attractive hotel and restaurant called **Hotel Posthaus Urigen.** It's handsomely decorated inside and out and advertises itself as a motorcycle meeting place. (Hotel Posthaus; CH-6465 Urigen; telephone 044/ 6 11 53.)

Near the bottom, on the northeast side of the Klausen in canton Glarus, are some narrow one-way cobblestoned tunnels. Traffic is controlled by a traffic light at each end.

Pragel Pass intersects with the road we're on in the town of

On the inside of a 180 on the Klausen Pass is the attractive Hotel Urigen. It advertises itself as a motorcycle meeting place.

Glarus, but it's so small and remote that there's no sign for it. Watch for a sign pointing to the left, west, to Klontal or Klontaler See (*Tal* attached to a German word means valley).

The road is two lanes as far as the lake, Klontaler See, where there's a modern terrace restaurant and hotel called **Rhodannenberg** (Hotel Rhodannenberg, CH-8750 Klontal, phone 058/ 617161). The rest of the road over the pass is one paved lane and has a feel like maybe nobody's ever been there. But a long period with no oncoming traffic doesn't mean there isn't a logging truck around the next corner. The asphalt is smooth but has a significant lip on each edge. It follows the lake for several kilometers, where there are triangular warning signs advising drivers to look out for frogs. Across the lake are sheer vertical cliffs of almost a thousand meters. Spectacular. Looks like Lake Louise at Banff in Canada.

Signs along the road with lengthy passages in German say that this part of the road is not open to traffic on weekends. The same signs greet the rider coming from the other direction across the pass at Muotatal, the valley on the other side. Muotatal leads down to Schwyz, the town the country's named after. (Heading for the Pragel from Schwyz, follow the signs to Muotatal, as there are none for the pass.)

Schwyz is the home of **Victorinox,** one of the "original Swiss Army Knife" factories. From Schwyz, the main road back toward Altdorf and Andermatt is called the Axenstrasse because it was carved by ax from the steep cliffs around Lake Luzern, Vierwaldstatter See.

Until recently, the Axenstrasse, hanging on the east side of the Vierwaldstatter See, was the only way around the lake toward the St. Gotthard. Now, there's a four-lane Autobahn tunnel through the cliffs on the other side of the lake, where before there was no road of any kind. (Following the lake in the opposite direction, actually west, from Schwyz, there's a ferry across the lake to Beckenried and connections with the roads of the Berner Oberland.)

A lesser pass, the Ibergeregg, 1406 meters and heading northeasterly, starts in the middle of Schwyz, by the church. The view over Vierwaldstatter See from the restaurant at the top is great. Little-trafficked and heavily forested, the Ibergeregg comes down by a couple of lakes and a huge pilgrimage church at Einsiedeln, not far from Zurich. The church is of modest historic or artistic interest, but it is big.

An even less challenging pass called Sattelegg, 1130 meters, loops east from the north end of Ibergeregg back toward Zurich See and civilization. Sattelegg has a pleasant restaurant, but an unpleasantly low speed limit.

West of
Andermatt

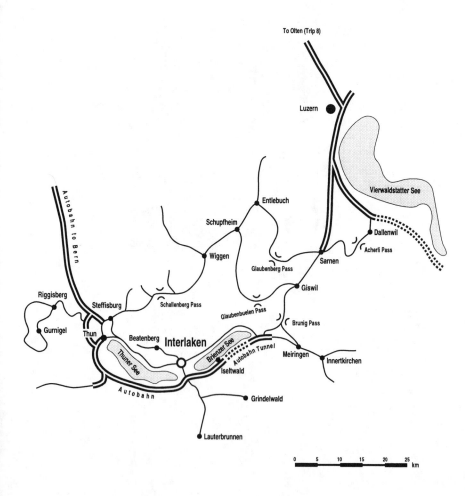

The Berner Oberland

West of Andermatt, west of the Furka and the Grimsel and the Susten, downstream from the Aareschlucht, in the valley of the Aare River, is the town of **Interlaken**. It's in canton Bern, in the area called the Berner Oberland, the high mountain country south of Switzerland's capital, Bern.

Interlaken is between two lakes made by the Aare River, the Brienzer See to the east and the Thuner See, to the west. It has been host to every guided tour that hits Switzerland. It's the jumping-off place for cog train rides up the Jungfrau mountain. It's also a great place to buy a Swiss army knife or a watch from Bucherer or a cup of genuine English tea. On one cross street into the old part of town, there's a hardware store (Eisenwaren) with everything from hand tools to Swiss cowbells. The saving grace of this tourist trap town is the public parking in front of most of the shops, and the good riding in the nearby mountains.

The area is crawling with hotels. There are big ones and little ones, expensive and cheap, in the bigger towns, on lakes, and hanging on the mountainside above little villages.

The island village of **Iseltwald,** one potential home base, hugs the cliffs on the south shore of Brienzer See. To get there, take the Autobahn around the south shore of the lake and take the exit (Ausfahrt) onto Iseltwald. Tourist Office, CH-3807 Iseltwald; phone 036/ 45 12 01.

A choice hotel right on the lake where the lake steamer stops is the **Strandhotel,** CH-3807 Iseltwald; phone 036/ 45 13 13; FAX 036/ 45 13 15. Upon exiting the freeway onto Iseltwald, there's a parking lot for tourists. The road into the village is marked with the international "do not enter" sign. But the little white sign underneath reads to the effect of, "unless you have business." So ride on in and have some business.

Another village with hotels, restaurants, and rooms for rent is **Beatenberg,** on the cliff hundreds of meters above the north shore of the Thuner See. Follow signs from the north side of Interlaken. From the whole village, there are sweeping views of Thuner Sea below and the Berner Oberland mountains beyond, including the Jungfrau. Beatenberg is a good place to catch Alpenglow, the almost hot pink glow of snow covered mountains in the rising or setting sun.

On the opposite shore of Brienzer See from Iseltwald is an outdoor museum called **Ballenberg** with a collection of farmhouses from all parts of Switzerland. Park and walk in.

Trip 5 Switzerland's Yosemite

· ·

Distance   *About 60 kilometers round trip from Interlaken*
Terrain   *Curving valley roads*
Highlights   *Spectacular cliffs, waterfalls, and glaciered mountains*

There's a dead end valley 12 kilometers south of Interlaken so breathtakingly beautiful, such a joy to behold, that it's worth a detour. It's called **Lauterbrunnen,** valley of the waterfalls. The valley is narrower than Yosemite, and has at least as many waterfalls, one inside the mountain, called **Trummelbach.** It's possible to stay in the valley. Two hotels are the **Schutzen;** phone 036/ 55 20 32; FAX 036/ 55 29 50; and the **Jungfrau;** phone 036/ 55 34 34; FAX 036/ 55 25 23; both addressed CH-3822 Lauterbrunnen. The latter has a good indoor pool.

A cable car from Lauterbrunnen goes up to the top of the **Schilthorn** mountain to what is reportedly the highest revolving restaurant in the world.

The road to Lauterbrunnen intersects with a road into the next valley east. It leads in just a few kilometers to the village of **Grindelwald.** Grindelwald is pretty touristy, but it's at the base of the **Eiger,** the mountain face that Clint Eastwood played on in the movie, *The Eiger Sanction.* It's handy to know that the Eiger, another word for "devil," is separated from the Jungfrau mountain, "the maiden," by a mountain called "Monk."

The tourist village of Grindelwald has another claim to the traveler's attention besides the Eiger. It's home to a "gotta have" hotel guide for the budget traveler in Switzerland called

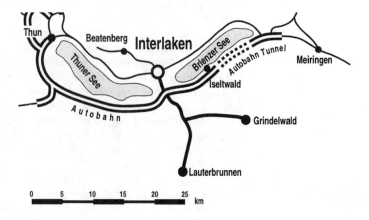

E and G Hotels. "E and G" stands for Einfach and Gemutlich, which loses something in the translation provided: "simple and cozy." It's published every year and lists 175 or so modestly priced hotels all over Switzerland. Each listing has a color picture along with prices, hours, address and phone, and a clever symbol system that describes showers, pools, views, and other amenities. Naturally, a cheaper hotel in the city may prove less attractive than one of similar price in the country. The book is available at all Swiss tourist offices, or write: E and G Hotels, CH-3818 Grindelwald, Switzerland; phone 036/ 53 44 88; FAX 036/ 53 44 84.

There are plenty of hotels in Grindelwald.

The Lauterbrunnen valley, known as the valley of the waterfalls—Switzerland's Yosemite—is located just a few kilometers from Interlaken. It is possible to stay right at the foot of Staubbach waterfall, shown here. The witch's hat church steeple is typical of German-speaking Switzerland. This is the countryside where all the tourists have fondue, some expressing surprise that it isn't always cheese.

Trip 6 North of Interlaken

· ·

Distance *About 180 kilometers from Interlaken via Glaubenberg Pass plus about 40 via Acherli Pass*

Terrain *Sweeping and twisting through meadows and forests on five lower passes, some narrow, tight stuff*

Highlights *Bucolic motorcycle favorite roads, a couple of motorcycle cafes, mostly off tourist routes, Schallenberg (1167 meters), Glaubenbuelen Pass (1611 meters), Glaubenberg Pass (1643 meters), Brunig Pass (1008 meters), Acherli Pass (1458 meters)*

This loop offers pleasant, bucolic, often challenging, but not exotic riding off the main tourist routes. Alpine guidebooks don't mention these roads.

The **Schallenberg road** starts climbing from the town of Thun, at the west end of the Thuner See, the westerly of the two lakes that bracket Interlaken. From the north side of Thun, signs direct you first to Steffisburg, then to Schallenberg. (The English ear doesn't distinguish between "burg" and "berg," but technically the former is a fortified town and the latter is a mountain.)

This is a sweeper road that has no great commercial or tourist value, so it's a motorcycle favorite. The area is a bit less polished-looking than most parts of Switzerland. The cafe at the top is almost exclusively aimed at serving *Tofflers*. All the

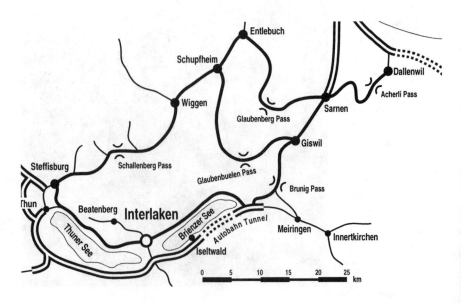

close-by parking is for motorcycles. A choice second-floor balcony lets patrons watch the road and the parking lot activity.

The east side of the Schallenberg comes down to a village called Wiggen. From Wiggen, the trip heads east in the direction of Luzern for a few kilometers. Just at the edge of a town called Schupfheim, a road to the right leads south to a town called Fluhli. This is the **Glaubenbuelen Pass** road, sometimes called "Panorama Strasse." The road is twisting, paved, one-lane across the top with lovely views of lakes and mountains and forests. But it seems like only cows are looking at the panorama. There are no restaurants, no services. The Swiss will insist that Heidi came from eastern Switzerland, but the Glaubenbuelen looks like what Heidi country ought to look like. In the fall and spring the road may be full of cows heading to or from the high pastures, with floral head dresses in the fall. In either case, the lead cow will wear a big brass bell hung from an elaborate collar. Lesser cows have smaller bells and smaller collars, down to the least with tin sheet metal bells.

The pass road connects with the main highway at Giswil just in time to climb over the Brunig Pass back toward Interlaken. (Looking for the Panorama Strasse from the Giswil side, the only hint is a sign on the main road in Giswil pointing to Schupfheim.)

To extend the trip, instead of going back to Interlaken over the Brunig, take the main road in the opposite direction toward Luzern. Then at Sarnen, head back north on the Glaubenberg Pass. More below.

The Brunig isn't high, but it *did* have some great sweepers that drew motorcycles from all around. A few years ago an avalanche took out most of the good sweepers and some vehicles with it. The replacement road does the job, but has less oomph. There remains one corner, a righthander going up from the east, that has a pull-out space that fills with bikes on good

The Schallenberg is a non-commercial, non-tourist, motorcycle favorite. The cafe at the top comes with special parking for bikes and a prize second floor balcony from which to watch the developing scene below.

days. And the several restaurants and hotels at the top often host huge crowds of motorcyclists. Friday night is supposed to be *the* night on the Brunig. The **Motel Restaurant Brunig** always has a sport bike mounted on a post out front, changed from time to time. Phone 036/ 711133; CH-6082 Brunig. The **Restaurant Silvana** has a big lot carved out of the mountain-side, often packed with bikes. Its front tables are right on the road for good view and sound. From the top of the Brunig, a dead end road goes south a few kilometers to some small villages with good views of the Aare valley.

Parallel to and east of the Glaubenbuelen Pass (the "Panorama Strasse") is another pass road called Glaubenberg. They must have named them to confuse us. Anyway, it's at least as high, even less used, and is also one-lane across the top. A restaurant/ski lodge named **Hotel Langis** on the south slope accommodates lots of motorcyclists during the summer. The north end of the Glaubenberg is in the middle of a village called Entlebuch, a few kilometers closer to Luzern than Schupfheim, above. Its southeast side ends at Sarnen, a town at the end of a lake by the same name.

From Sarnen it's possible to cross the main road and catch an obscure pass called Acherli over the next mountain into the Engelberg valley. There are no signs for the pass, so follow the signs from Sarnen to Kerns and then Wisserlen. This will be the little pass road. Persist. There may be some cattle gates to open (and close). The pass ends on the Engelberg road at Dallenwil. There are no services on the pass, but it isn't far.

From the Engelberg road it's only a few kilometers on the Autobahn toward the St. Gotthard to **Beckenried,** where a ferry crosses the Vierwaldstatter See to the roads of Trip 4 out of Andermatt. Or head back to Interlaken over the Brunig. The west side of the Brunig has a connection over toward the Susten Pass and Grimsel Pass. Weekend bikers often head that way.

Even though some of its famous sweepers were swept away by a recent avalanche, Brunig Pass has always been popular. The Motel Restaurant Brunig, atop the pass, is a "Tofftreftpunkt," a motorcycle meeting place.

Trip 7 Gurnigel

Distance	*About 120 kilometers, round trip from Interlaken*
Terrain	*Lakeside road, then a climb through woods to high pasture*
Highlights	*Handsome lakefront, woods, maybe military artillery, Gurnigel Pass (1608 meters)*

Riggisberg, about 15 kilometers northwest of the town of Thun, is the access key to a loop west of the Thuner See. From Riggisberg, this loop heads south on back roads to the summit at a restaurant called **Berghaus Gurnigel.** The easterly leg of the loop is a full two-lane road. The westerly leg is partly one-lane and is a bit rough, although paved. Both are fun. Both have good views, as does the restaurant at the top. The restaurant terrace has views over the low mountains to the south, often used for military exercises.

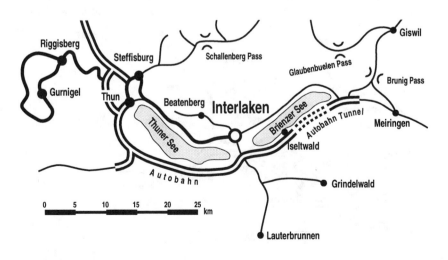

Trip 8 Trimbach bei Olten

Distance	*About 140 kilometers, one way from Interlaken*
Terrain	*Highway and Autobahn*
Highlights	*Thousands and thousands of motorcycles*

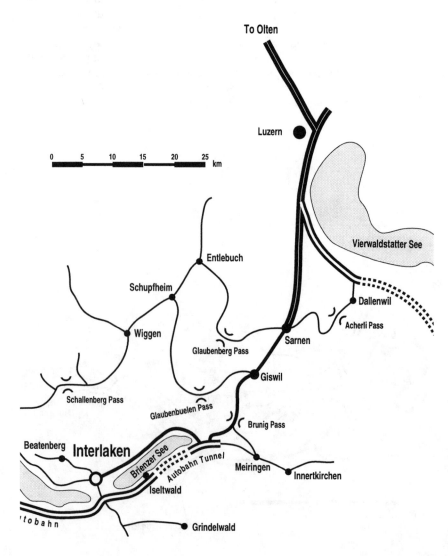

Friday night is the meeting night on Brunig Pass, but the biggest gathering of riders is usually on Thursday night at Trimbach bei Olten (Trimbach is just north of Olten), about 80 kilometers straight north of Interlaken, south of Basel, and west of Zurich. To get to Trimbach bei Olten from Interlaken, head north over the Brunig Pass and continue on the autostrada past Luzern. Olten is just off the autobahn, about halfway between Luzern and Basel.

A huge parking lot next to a modest Gasthaus named **Eisenbahn** (railroad) accommodates about 3,000 motorcycles, and on good nights they spill out over neighboring fields. No events. No program. Only tire kicking. Special parking is reserved for any and all Harleys. The latest everything will show up, along with customized and restored bikes of all kinds. Every Thursday. Unfortunately, there aren't any recommended hotels nearby. There are a couple of serviceable ones in Olten.

On Thursday nights, thousands of motorcyclists gather for tire kicking at the Eisenbahn restaurant in the Swiss village of Trimbach bei Olten. Bikes fill the parking lot, and the rest spill over adjoining fields and roads.

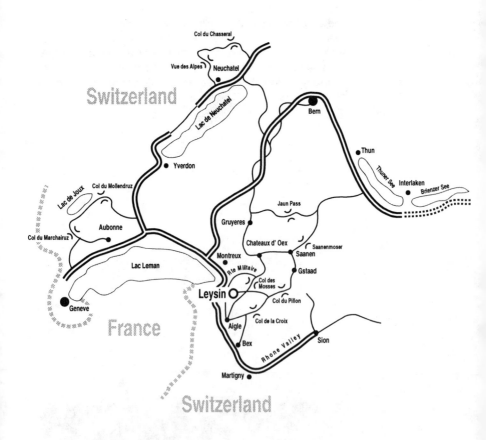

Leysin

Hung on a mountainside at about 1200 meters, **Leysin** is a village with a view and a lot of hotels, and it's off the beaten track. It's in canton Vaud, and French, *s'il vous plait*. From most any point on the one road through town, from any balcony on any hotel, and from any terrace, there's a view across the Valley of the Rhone River (that started at the glacier on the Furka Pass) to the eternal snows of Mont Blanc and its neighbors.

Leysin is about six kilometers off the Col des Mosses road, the one road into Leysin, above the Rhone Valley town of Aigle. A cog train runs down the mountain from Leysin to Aigle.

A small family-run hotel near the top of the town, with views and good hearty cooking, is the **Hotel Mont Riant,** CH-1854 Leysin-Feydey; phone 025/ 34 27 01; Fax 025/ 34 27 04.

Another is **Hotel Colina,** CH-1854 Leysin; phone 025/ 34 10 12.

Since there's a Swiss hotel school in Leysin, there are many other hotels, some quaint and some more grand. In case you need a wash cloth, there's even a Holiday Inn.

Trip 9 Simmental and Jaun Pass

Distance	*About 145 kilometers from Interlaken to Leysin via Jaun Pass; about 110 kilometers via Saanenmoser*
Terrain	*Easy sweeping climbs over low passes*
Highlights	*Picturesque villages and covered bridges, lush pastures, forest, medieval walled town and famous cheese factory (Gruyeres), Jaun Pass (1509 meters), Saanenmoser (1279 meters)*

The picturesque Simmental (valley) feeds into the south shore of the Thuner See, just west of Interlaken. From the lake, the road up the valley winds past quaint wooden covered bridges and through small villages. Unfortunately, it's marked "no passing" (double white, not double yellow) for practically its whole length. And the many little villages are famous for strict enforcement of speed limits.

Up the Simmental about 15 kilometers from the Thuner See is a tiny one-building village called **Weissenburg** (don't confuse it with Weissenbach, farther upstream). The building is the **Hostellerie Alte Post** at Weissenburg, a joy for any antique connoisseur as well as anyone ready for a genuine Swiss meal. It's famous for serving coffee cream in chocolate cups that melt in the coffee.

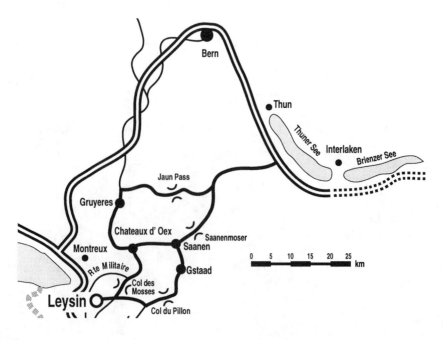

The top of the Simmental is called Saanenmoser, not much of a pass, but it leads right into one of Switzerland's toniest tourist areas: **Gstaad.** *Everybody* skis and tennises here, or at least the rich and famous are supposed to.

From Gstaad, it's straight over the Col de Pillon to Leysin, or from nearby Saanen, it's straight ahead over the Col des Mosses to Leysin. Both of these roads are more completely described in Trip 10. The road up the mountain to Leysin is just about where the Col de Pillon road and the Col des Mosses road meet.

But should you choose the longer route over the Jaun Pass, the turnoff is out in the country, in a meadow, just outside the little Simmental village of Reidenbach. Jaun Pass (yawn, not whawn) runs between the Simmental on the east and Gruyeres on the west with views of the Simmental. It's an easy climb and there's a restaurant at the top of the pass.

Gruyeres, on the west end of the Jaun Pass, is a preserved old walled city on a hill. No vehicles. It's worth the short walk in to visit. Bikes can park right by the city gate. Too many restaurants offer almost any concoction or most any kind of berry with the thickest, richest cream imaginable, cream that comes from the cheese factory for which the town is known. The factory is at the bottom of the hill and is open to visitors in the morning. The language in Gruyeres is French.

South from Gruyeres is the Col des Mosses, leading to the road to Leysin.

Trip 10 Three Cols and a Route

Distance	*About 144 kilometers from Leysin*
Terrain	*Fun sweepers over lower passes, mostly modern highways, modest height and difficulty*
Highlights	*Well known resorts (Gstaad, Chateau d'Oex), log village (Saanen), German/French culture border, Col du Pillon (1546 meters), ★ Col de la Croix (1778 meters), Col des Mosses (1445 meters), Route Militaire*

The Col des Mosses climbs out of the Rhone Valley from Aigle, past a handsome private castle, and past the dead end road to Leysin.

Chateau d'Oex (sounds like "shat oh day") and **Rougemont** are attractive tourist towns at the north end of the Col des Mosses. The medieval church at Rougemont is worth a stop if you're passing by. Although the village is French, the church is of Germanic style, because the diocese was controlled from nearby Saanen.

An interesting and fun alternate route parallels the Col des Mosses from Aigle. It's a military road and is open only on Saturdays, Sundays, and holidays. The south end, out of the valley village of Corbeyrier climbs through handsome vineyards, then some narrow, steep hairpins and a twisting, one-way-at-a-time tunnel.

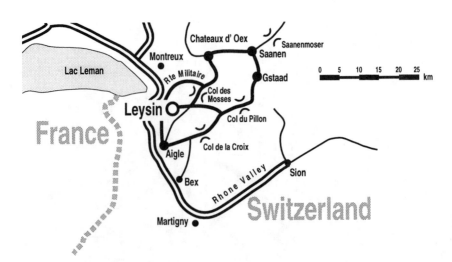

The north end cruises by a lake, then over many bridges. Some pass roads number the hairpins. This one numbers the bridges: forty some. Unfortunately, part of the road has a low speed limit.

At the lovely log house village of **Saanen** (also the westerly base of the Sannenmoser) the road heads south for **Gstaad,** and then starts climbing the Col du Pillon through the village of **Gsteig,** which has one of the nicer Germanic-Swiss church steeples, shaped much like a witch's hat.

The pass out of Gsteig is the Col du Pillon. As the name implies, the top of the pass is in French-speaking Switzerland. In the few kilometers between Gsteig and the top of the pass, the buildings and menus change from Germanic to French.

The attractive restaurant at the top of the Col du Pillon, with a terrace viewing the highest peaks in the area, is called **Les Diablerets.** So are the peaks. So is the next town. At the next town, Les Diablerets, the Col de la Croix road heads southwest. Somehow, the Col de la Croix is uncluttered, with sweeping turns and sweeping views. It has gotten rough in spots. The Col road comes down to the village of **Villars,** one of the few Swiss towns that's anxious to sell condos to foreigners.

At Villars, the road forks. One leg heads for the Rhone Valley at Aigle. One winds down to the valley at Bex. From either, it's just a few kilometers back up the Col des Mosses road to Leysin.

Trip 11 North of Lac Leman

Distance	*About 280 kilometers round trip from Leysin*
Terrain	*Some autoroute, farm land, lower wooded passes*
Highlights	*Good views of Lac Leman, Lac du Joux, winding roads through woods, French culture, Col du Marchairuz (1447 meters), Col du Mollendruz (1180 meters), Col du Chasseral (1502 meters)*

Arcing west from Leysin and Aigle for about 100 kilometers, the north shore of Lac Leman harbors the major cities of French-speaking Switzerland: Montreux, Lausanne, and at the west end, Geneve (Geneva). Suspended above the lake, sometimes on spectacular viaducts, an autoroute (freeway) whisks right by the **Castle of Chillon** (made famous by Lord Byron's poem) on the east end of the lake to Geneva on the west end.

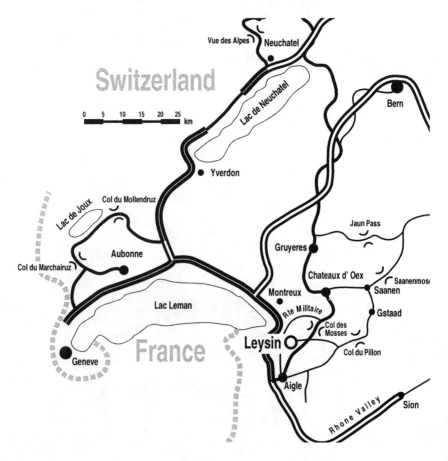

The Castle of Chillon is a real medieval castle that seems to rise right out of Lac Leman. It can be visited and it's accessible from the lake shore road below the autoroute, just west of the city of Montreux.

North of the lake and autoroute are two passes that are good riding if you're in the area. Both are surprisingly rural. Both lead to a nice lake, Lac du Joux, that is relatively uncluttered. **Col du Marchairuz** goes inland, north, from the autoroute exit "Aubonne," to the westerly end of the Lac du Joux, and **Col du Mollendruz** goes southeast from the easterly end of the lake.

To get to these passes, it's best to avoid traffic along the lake shore road by taking the autoroute west toward Geneve (Geneva), past Lausanne, exiting at Aubonne, then climbing northwest over the Col du Marchairuz. The col road descends to the Lac du Joux. Follow either shore to the east end of the lake, and then climb south over the Col du Mollendruz.

From the south end of the Col du Mollendruz, head east toward Yverdon on Lac du Neuchatel, and follow the north shore of the lake to the town of Neuchatel. At Neuchatel, the Vue des Alpes road climbs north toward St. Imier, where the Col des Pontins leads to the Col du Chasseral.

From the Col du Chasseral, autoroutes lead south to Montreux and Leysin.

Cobblestones like these remain only on short historic pieces of road. These cobblestones help preserve the atmosphere in front of the Castle of Chillon on Lac Leman (Lake Geneva). The castle was made famous in English literature by Lord Byron's poem, The Prisoner of Chillon. *The nearby autoroute (freeway) is fast and smooth.*

Switzerland

Col du Sanetsch

Autostrada

Lötschental

Brig

Visp

Sion

Rhone Valley

Simplon Pass

Martigny

Tasch

Saas Almagell

to Italy

Col de la Forclaz

Col des Planches

Zermatt

France

Champex

Matterhorn/
Monte Cervino

Chamonix

Breuil-Cervinia

Flumet

Tunnel

Grand St. Bernard

Italy

Mt. Blanc

Pre St. Didier

Col des Saisies

La Thuile

Morgex

Chatillon

Colle San Carlo

Aosta

Autostrada to Torino

Petit St. Bernard

Col de Pre

Cormet de Roselend

Bourg St. Maurice

Gran Paradiso

0   5   10   15   20   25
km

Cogne

The Rhone Valley makes a 90-degree bend at a pretty good sized Swiss town called **Martigny.** Quite French. It's where two pass roads head out to encircle the eternal snows of the highest mountain in the Alps, Mont Blanc, 4807 meters (15779 feet!). From Martigny the Col de la Forclaz road heads toward France, and the Grand St. Bernard road heads toward Italy.

Martigny, or any of the villages hung on the mountains around it, are good bases for the Mont Blanc trip. Right where the two pass roads come together in Martigny is a hotel called **La Porte d'Octodure;** CH-1921 Martigny-Croix; phone 026/ 22 71 21; FAX 026/ 22 21 73. *Malhereusement,* it's a Best Western!

A little village called **Les Marecottes,** atop a spectacular road just eight kilometers from the Martigny town square, has a variety of hotels that have served motorcyclists well. Go northwest from the square, over a covered wooden bridge, and keep climbing. Part of the road is modern, part is one lane, precariously hanging on the edge of the Gorge du Trient. One hotel is called **Aux Mille Etoiles;** CH-1923 Les Marecottes; phone 026/ 6 16 66.

From the autoroute in the Rhone Valley, the pass roads are signed via a bypass road that misses downtown Martigny.

From the Swiss side of the Col du Grand St. Bernard, the restaurant in sunny Italy is almost at hand. Across the border in those buildings there will be cappucino and fresh pasta.

Trip 12　Valley of the Rhone

Distance	*About 160 kilometers between Martigny and Andermatt, one way; about 110 kilometers between Martigny and Tasch (Zermatt), one way; about 100 kilometers between Martigny and Simplon Pass, one way*
Terrain	*Fairly straight valley road and sweeping mountain climbs on good modern highway*
Highlights	*Sweep up a finger valley toward the Matterhorn, over a high mountain pass (★ Simplon, at 2006 meters), some concrete roofed highway*

From the high passes at Andermatt, the Rhone Valley makes a pretty straight shot down to Martigny. The higher eastern part of the valley, called the Goms, is an amusing ride through log cabin villages. The lower part is more commercial and boring. It does make a functional east-west connection, about 150 kilometers long, with such high mountains on both sides that there's hardly any way out. From the Grimsel Pass back by Andermatt, there's no through road going north until the Col des Mosses by Leysin. It is possible to put a bike or car on a train and take it through a tunnel toward Interlaken. Switzerland is slowly extending an Autobahn autoroute up the valley.

Two dead end roads north make for interesting escapes into high valleys: Lotschental climbs up to the glaciers behind Lauterbrunnen (turn off at the signs for the train tunnel to Goppenstein), and the Col du Sanetsch from Sion almost makes it across the top to Gsteig, but doesn't.

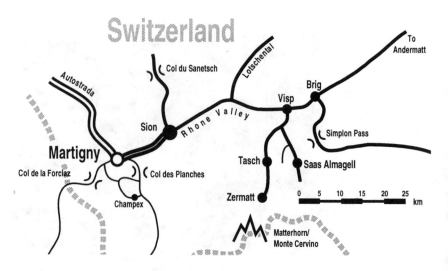

One road out of the Rhone Valley to the south toward Italy, the ★ **Simplon Pass,** starts at Brig, 50 kilometers below the Furka. The Simplon is one of the major passes of the Alps between Italy and France, through Switzerland. The first major Alpine train tunnel went under the Simplon to carry the Orient Express. Both sides of the pass road are in Switzerland, with good quality sweepers to the summit on both sides. The north side has an amazing "S" curved poured concrete suspension bridge. On the summit is a giant stone eagle monument and a couple of serviceable restaurants. One regular menu item is goulash soup, a spicy, meaty specialty of the Germanic Alps that tastes something like chili.

Near **Brig,** there's a fairly good sized bike shop in the adjoining village of Naters, right beside the road east toward the Furka.

(For good road connections from the south side of the Simplon, see the chapter "Alps South of Andermatt, Ticino Connections.")

Several dead end valleys go south from the Rhone Valley. The most famous valley is **Mattertal** to **Zermatt** and the **Matterhorn,** but no vehicles are allowed into Zermatt. The Rhone Valley turnoff for Zermatt and the Mattertal is at Visp. It's a fine sweeping ride up the Mattertal as far as Tasch, where one of the biggest parking lots in Europe accommodates tourists taking the cog train the rest of the way to Zermatt. There is underground and indoor parking at Tasch. Outdoor bike parking is available right next to the train station.

The village of **Randa,** just below Tasch, bears witness to the terror of the Alps. In recent years a whole mountain collapsed into the valley, burying everything—the stream, parts of the village, the road and railroad—under granite boulders. The road and railroad now go around the site.

The east fork of the intersection in the road up the Mattertal goes all the way up to the towns of **Saas Fee** and **Saas Almagell.** The road to the former is interesting, with glaciers right at hand, but it's a walk-around-only village. Motorcycle parking is free.

Just downstream from Visp in the Rhone Valley, without a sign, everything changes from German to French: architecture, menus, bread, even cars.

Sion is a large city with motorcycle shops that speak French. Visible from the valley road near Sion are military airplane hangars in the mountainside and airstrips alongside the road.

Trip 13 All Around Mont Blanc

Distance	*About 300 kilometers from Martigny*
Terrain	*Circle the greatest mountain in the Alps, Mont Blanc; from low valleys with some congestion, climb to empty mountain roads; three major Alpine passes and several lesser ones; some narrow, tight, steep hairpins.*
Highlights	*Three countries, famous passes and ski resorts, Roman ruins, plus some quiet, remote, twisting stuff, Champex, Col des Planches, ★ Col du Grand St. Bernard (2469 meters), Colle San Carlo (1971 meters), Col du Petit St. Bernard (2188 meters), ★ ★ Cormet de Roselend (1922 meters), Col du Pre (1703 meters), Col des Saisies (1633 meters), Chamonix Col des Montets (1461 meters), Col de la Forclaz (1526 meters)*

Two amusing little roads start near the Hotel La Porte d'Octodure in Martigny. Just toward downtown a few hundred meters, a tiny road, the **Col des Planches,** climbs up the mountainside. It isn't high, but it does lead up and over to a high resort at **Verbier,** 1390 meters. Up the **Grand St. Bernard** a few kilometers, at **Les Valettes,** another small road makes a twisting climb up to a mountain lake village called **Champex.**

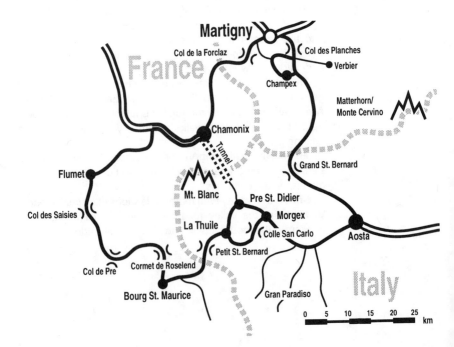

The road goes through and winds back down to the Grand St. Bernard road at **Orsieres,** where an interesting dead end valley road, **Val Ferret,** heads up toward some glaciers at 1705 meters.

There are two St. Bernard Passes, a Grand (big) and a Petit or Piccolo (little) St. Bernard. The big one goes between Martigny, Switzerland, and Aosta, Italy. It's where the dogs are. The little one goes from Aosta in Italy to France. There's a statue of St. Bernard on both of them.

The ★ **Grand St. Bernard Pass** is fairly commercial and has high-speed sweepers so well engineered that it's hard to realize how quickly you're up among the glaciers. But it goes by tunnel into Italy. Motorcycles want to stay on the pass road, so turn off just after entering the tunnel, where a sign, "Col," points to the right. At the top, the restaurant on the Italian side is more pleasant than the Swiss one. The Swiss one will have sandwiches and cold cuts; the Italian, fresh pasta and salad and cappuccino. Most of the dogs around are stuffed toys. On the Italian side, the 14 kilometers between the pass and the Italian entrance to the tunnel are fairly challenging and wild. Approaching the pass from Italy, the pass road leaves the tunnel road just before a long viaduct that leads to the tunnel entrance. There's a place to change money at the complex of offices just across the viaduct. Italian lira are needed for cash purchases in Italy. The rest of the route down into Aosta has commercial traffic.

Aosta center has some significant **Roman ruins,** an arch, walls, and a theater. On the east end of town, past the airport, is a very large motorcycle shop called America. It does not sell Harleys.

Beaufort cheese on the hoof, high on the Cormet de Roselend, one of France's over-looked passes. Cows use the road to reach high pastures in the spring, and to come down in the fall. You'll know if you come up behind them, as they leave a well marked trail.

Even though it's in a fabulous Alpine valley, Aosta has too much traffic and smog to love. There are a couple of dead end valleys that lead up into interesting high country (see Trip 14, "Val D'Aosta").

To get to the Piccolo St. Bernard Pass from Aosta, follow the signs to Courmayeur and the Italian entrance to what used to be the longest vehicle tunnel in the world under Mont Blanc. Commercial truck traffic to the tunnel is terrible. An elaborate autostrada is under construction, but . . . Fortunately, motorcyclists need not go through the tunnel. From the smog-filled highway there are occasional glimpses of Mont Blanc, huge and white, before the turnoff at the village of Pre St. Didier, 30 kilometers from Aosta, where the Piccolo St. Bernard goes south and leaves the traffic behind.

Before the Piccolo St. Bernard turnoff at Pre St. Didier, there's a long cut over an obscure pass called the Colle San Carlo. It's recently been improved with new retaining walls and pavement. Escape the traffic early by turning up the Colle at a village called Morgex. The pass isn't marked. The sign is to Arpy, a town on the pass. After a great climb twisting through the forests, the road descends into the village of La Thuile, on the Piccolo St. Bernard road.

The rest of the Italian side of the Piccolo St. Bernard is a delight. Often the road cuts through deep banks of snow well into mid-June. The only village, La Thuile, has a good ristorante called **Grotto,** and another called **Les Marmottes** just across from the little and only parking lot in town. Try tortellini carne in garlic and walnut sauce.

Sometimes on the Piccolo St. Bernard there is nobody around to check traffic out of Italy or into France, and no place to change money. Banks at Bourg St. Maurice, the closest town of note in France, close at noon. Fortunately, the only restaurants, on the French side, will usually take Swiss or French francs or Italian lira. And even remote gas stations and restaurants in France take credit cards.

Some American motorcyclists have noted that French road repair crews use a lot of gravel, often marked with a portable sign that profiles a pre-World War II Citroen spraying rocks from its wheels. Gravel piles almost always spoil the French side of the Grand St. Bernard.

One of the *plus joli* (prettiest) roads in France, the ★ ★ **Cormet de Roselend** (sounds like "core may"), starts at Bourg St. Maurice at the base of the Petit (it's *petit* in France, not *piccolo*) St. Bernard. Find it heading north from the east end of town. The road has no commercial or even ski activity. Early in the season, it may be marked *ferme* (closed) because of snow. Give it a try. Very possibly a bike can get through. Parts are only one lane wide and bumpy, but it feels like no one else was ever there. Near the top should be herds of handsome red-brown cows, source of the famous cheese that comes from the other side of the mountain at Beaufort.

On the north side of the Cormet is a beautiful lake with a couple of satisfactory mountain restaurants. The northerly one is a bit more substantial in building and menu. The lake results from a dam (*barrage* in French) with a road across the top that leads to another pass of no significance except views so wonderful that even the most enthusiastic rider will pause to look. It's mostly one lane wide, paved, and is called **Col du Pre.** There is a restaurant on it. Then, it winds down into the town of cheese, **Beaufort.**

Three kilometers below Beaufort the **Col des Saisies** (sounds like "coal day sigh zee") road comes in. Cross country skiing events for the Albertville Olympics were held at the Col des Saisies. It's a north/south pass, with the north end daylighting at Flumet, a little village on a valley road that leads toward Megeve and Chamonix.

There is a more obscure way down. At one of the several traffic circles installed for the Olympics, turn north. The little road winds through forests to a little village, Crest Voland. The road is not marked but I encourage you to explore.

Coming into **Chamonix,** all traffic gets funneled onto an autoroute that marches up the valley on stilts out over the top of everything. Finally, at Chamonix, the huge glaciers of Mont Blanc come into view. And the tunnel entrance to Italy. Chamonix is a summer and winter tourist center with all the accommodations and traffic to prove it. One of the most exotic cable car rides (*telepherique* in French) in the world goes from Chamonix to the **Aiguille du Midi** on the Mont Blanc massif. From the main highway through the city, an underpass takes you to the parking lot of the cable car. The ride up is exciting if the weather's clear.

Most of the traffic is going through the tunnel to Italy, not to Switzerland. For Switzerland, follow the signs to Argentiere and Col des Montets, a hardly noticeable pass, and on to the Swiss border.

The Swiss side of the border crossing has all kinds of services, including money exchanges. Across the border there's a turnoff to a town called Finhaut. A road climbs through Finhaut to dead-end at a lake called **Emosson** at 1930 meters. The road's good and there's a restaurant with a terrace and view of the whole Mont Blanc massif.

Back at the foot of the mountain, the road on to Martigny climbs over the Col de la Forclaz. The Martigny side of this col has a couple of restaurants with good views of the Rhone Valley and surrounding vineyards.

Trip 14   Val d'Aosta

Distance	*About 78 kilometers from Martigny to Aosta, one way, plus about 50 kilometers from Aosta to Breuil (the Matterhorn, called Monte Cervino in Italy) one way, plus about 25 kilometers from Aosta to any of the valleys in the Parco Nazionale Gran Paradiso, one way*
Terrain	*Once out of the Aosta valley, quiet, twisting narrow roads into high forgotten valleys surrounded by glaciers*
Highlights	*As close to the Matterhorn as a road goes, plus a natural National Park of glaciers and mountain peaks*

Just west of Aosta, on the traffic-jammed highway toward Courmayeur (the Mont Blanc tunnel), three roads head south into the **Parco Nazionale Gran Paradiso.** All dead-end. The closest to Aosta is Val di Cogne, the next is Val Savaranche, and the third, Val di Rhemes. They quickly leave traffic and civilization behind. Each twists and climbs into high Alpine valleys.

Val di Cogne is a good base for hikers and climbers and offers beautiful views of Mont Blanc and the Gran Paradiso.

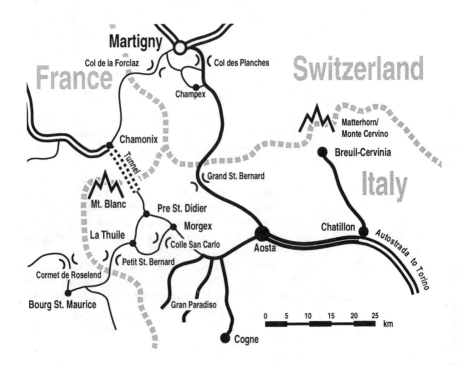

Twenty-six kilometers from Aosta, going east on the autostrada toward Torino, at Chatillon, a road climbs north to 2006 meters and the very base of the Matterhorn. Of course, in Italia, it's **Monte Cervino.** The village at the base, **Breuil,** has a lot of ski hotels, usually closed in the summer.

Just short of the end of the road is a little lake, **Lago Bleu.** Climb up over a little slope to see a picture to treasure . . . Cervino reflected in the lake.

The backside of the Matterhorn, the Italian side, where it's known as Monte Cervino, is best viewed across little Lago Bleu at Breuil.

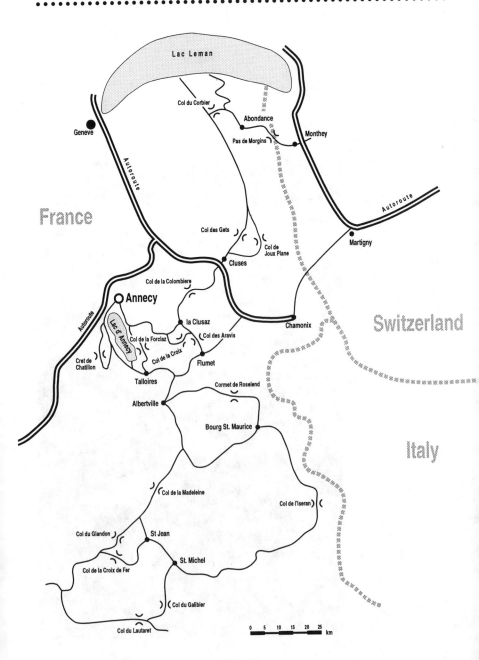

Lac d'Annecy

In France, south of Mont Blanc, are some of the highest passes and wildest country of the Alps. Exciting to explore. The '92 Olympics at Albertville highlighted some of them. France alone of the Alpine countries has good, prominently marked route numbers.

Although they're pretty well developed for winter sports, the French Alps seem to close down during the summer season. Facilities, almost endless in number and variety elsewhere in the Alps, are a bit harder to locate in France, and some pass roads aren't open until late in June.

But facilities are always open at **Lac d'Annecy,** one of the loveliest lakes in the Alps, just a few kilometers northwest of Albertville. Passes south of Lac Leman lead to Annecy, as do the autoroutes south from Geneve and west from Chamonix. The French province that includes Annecy and most of these good passes is Haute Savoie. Its flag looks almost like the Swiss flag.

The town of **Annecy,** at the north end of the lake, has all services, including a variety of large and helpful motorcycle shops, even Harley. (Several are located on the road leading toward Aix les Bains.)

Hotels for all tastes are located around the lake. On the eastern shore is a village called Talloires (say "Tal whar"). Besides some starred (by Michelin) and pricey places like **George Bis** and **Le Cottage,** F-74290 Talloires, phone 50/ 60 71 10; there's **Hotel le Lac,** fairly pretentious, phone 50/ 60 71 08, FAX 50/ 60 72 99, whose owner is a biker; **Hotel la Charpenterie,** attractive and more modest, phone 50/ 60 70 47, FAX 50/ 60 79 07; and **Hotel Beau Site,** phone 50/ 60 71 04.

Trip 15 Lac d'Annecy

Distance	*About 230 kilometers from Martigny to Annecy, one way*
Terrain	*Sweeping and twisting over seven non-commercial passes*
Highlights	*Farms, forests, high meadows, some narrow roads, ski resorts, Pas de Morgins (1369 meters), Col du Corbier (1237 meters), Col des Gets (1163 meters), Col de Joux Plane (1712 meters), Col de la Colombiere (1613 meters), Col des Aravis (1486 meters), Col de la Croix Fry (1467 meters)*

Several passes south of Lac Leman make a fun connection with Annecy and the roads of the French Alps. On most of them there is no traffic. Start out of the Rhone Valley in Switzerland on the **Pas de Morgins.** From the town of Monthey, just a few kilometers downstream from Martigny, it climbs through

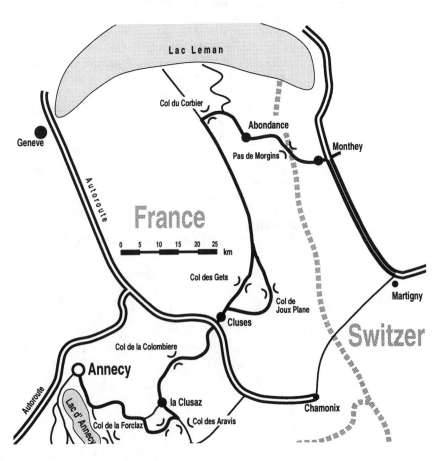

pleasant Swiss countryside and crosses into France at the top. The operator of the motorcycle shop in Monthey is an enthusiast who has biked all over the world, including North America and Baja.

Coming down into France below the town of Abondance, the little pass road of **Col du Corbier** heads up and south into a wonderful set of switchbacks on the northeast side. It leads to the next valley and the road up the **Col des Gets.** To the east of Gets is another little pass road called **Col de Joux Plane.** It's a one-lane road that twists up from the town of Morzine on the north to Samoens on the south. It's not conspicuously marked at either end, but it's popular with French and Swiss motorcyclists and is worth the effort to find it. There is a restaurant at the top.

All this leads down to a fairly large city, Cluses, on the autoroute toward Chamonix. Signing through Cluses is circuitous.

Across the autoroute from Cluses, the Col de la Colombiere leads up and over the mountains toward Annecy through St. Jean de Sixt and Thones. Colombiere is a noncommercial play road. Oil spills have been noted, though. There is a restaurant at the top.

From Flumet, on the loop around Mont Blanc (north end of the Col des Saisies), the Col des Aravis goes up and over toward Annecy. The Col des Aravis has a nice restaurant with a terrace view of Mont Blanc. Just down a little on the north side of the Col des Aravis, near the ski resort of **la Clusaz,** the Col de la Croix Fry heads up and west. It's a good road with little traffic, and a nice hotel restaurant complex on the west slope named after the pass, **La Croix Fry;** F-74230 Manigod; phone 50/ 44 90 16; FAX 50/ 44 90 28. The hotel has an outdoor pool. The Col de la Croix Fry leads to the town of Thones, and the main road to Annecy.

Col de Joux Plane, a narrow, obscure, fun pass in France, attracts a gathering of Harley riders. It is not well marked, but is worth finding.

Trip 16 South of Lac d'Annecy

Distance	*About 400 kilometers round trip from Annecy (shorter trip possible)*
Terrain	*From commercial valleys to mountain highs on every kind of paved road, limited facilities*
Highlights	*Ski resorts, two of the highest and loneliest roads of the Alps (★ ★ Col de l'Iseran, 2769 meters, and ★ ★ Col du Galibier, 2645 meters), Cret de Chatillon (1699 meters), Col de la Forclaz (1150 meters), ★ Col de la Madeleine (1984 meters), Col du Lautaret (2058 meters), Col du Glandon (1951 meters), Col de la Croix de Fer (2068 meters)*

Col de la Forclaz (same name as the pass out of Martigny, Switzerland) climbs right up the mountainside out of Talloires. In just a few kilometers, the restaurants at the summit provide views of the lake and of Talloires far below, as well as lunch, hang gliding, and parasailing.

78

Across the lake, the Cret de Chatillon climbs right out of Annecy. In seconds the road is out of traffic and in the woods. Above the woods, there are views across the lake to Mont Blanc.

Some of the highest and most awesome passes of the Alps are south of Albertville, but their lower slopes are less forested and the heights seem grayer. In fact, they are often called the Gray Alps. Civilization seems further removed. And it is. The Col de l'Iseran, named after the Isere River and its valley, the Val d'Isere (the river is *L'Isere* in French, so it sounds like "lee zayer," and the pass sounds like "coal duh lee zay rahn"), is the highest. The valley is where all the great skiing events took place in the Albertville Olympics, in a region made famous by earlier Olympic great Jean-Claude Killy. To reach the pass from Albertville, either follow the river upstream, or take the scenic high-cut route over the Cormet de Roselend to Bourg St. Maurice and Seez, and on up the valley. The valley from Albertville is sort of a truck route, relieved somewhat by the autoroute built for the Olympics.

The ski center at Val d'Isere, about 86 km from Albertville, looks naked and uninviting in the summer, with its concrete high rises set in big gravel parking lots, and most everything closed down. Above the ski center though, the road climbs and climbs through beautiful and ever-wilder looking country. As the deep snows melt in early summer, the meadows are carpeted with flowers. The south side, into the valley of the Arc River, seems stark and wilder still. There are no services on the pass.

The run down the valley of the Arc River between the south base of the Col de l'Iseran and north portal to the Col du Galibier at St. Michel is uninspiring. Then from St. Michel, the Col du Galibier climbs southerly over a hump, called Col du Telegraphe, before the really high stuff. It's much like Col de l'Iseran in its unoccupied isolation.

The south end of the Col du Galibier is the top of the Col du Lautaret, where services are on-again-off-again. From that intersection, loop west toward Grenoble, down to the village of Rochetaillee. Rochetaillee is the junction of the west end of the Col du Lautaret and the south end of the Col du Glandon. Head north on the Col du Glandon road to its summit, which happens to be the junction with the Col de la Croix de Fer. Straight ahead, north, the Col du Glandon road heads down to the Arc valley, while the Col de la Croix de Fer jogs east and a bit higher before working down to the Arc, ten kilometers farther upstream.

The north end of the Col du Glandon in the Arc valley is the south end of the Col de la Madeleine. Cross the valley and head up and over the Col de la Madeleine toward Albertville. There is a restaurant atop the Col de la Madeleine.

The Southern Alps

A succession of kings and emperors pushed the French border east across the southern Alps at the expense of Italy, so that almost all of the high country is in France today. A few minor passes cross down into Italy. The countryside is bleak and the few towns are walled fortresses, left over from the defense budgets of past centuries. Here are some of the highest passes in the Alps, several of which are known today as the Route des Grandes Alpes. The first Napoleon is supposed to have come this route when he landed in France from exile on the Mediterranean island of Elba. Taking these highest roads, he escaped detection until he was ready to pounce on Paris. It must have been quite a trip in 1815. We know that 100 days later, he was defeated at Waterloo and got shipped off a bit farther than Elba.

While the northern Alps abound in tourist accommodations, restaurants and hotels are few and far between in the southern Alps, and often closed. The small village of **Guillestre,** at 1000 meters, offers the best amenities. It's one of those fortress towns with stone works that boggle the mind, left over from Louis XIV. Guillestre is south of Briancon and east of Gap, and the base of two passes on the Route des Grandes Alpes, the Col de Vars and the Col d'Izoard. **Les Barnieres** is a good modern hotel with a good restaurant, even tennis and a pool in season (F-05600 Guillestre; phone 92/ 45 04 87). No English!

The Col d'Izoard, between Briancon and Guillestre, is full of strange formations. Napoleon slept here. (The bikes are parked off the paved road.)

Trip 17 Around Guillestre

Distance	*About 90 kilometers north over Col d'Izoard; about 280 south*
Terrain	*High, rugged mountains and roads, limited facilities*
Highlights	*Exotic wild scenery, Col d'Izoard (2361 meters), Col de Vars (2111 meters), Col du Restefond (2678 meters), Col de la Cayolle (2327 meters), Col d'Allos (2240 meters)*

The Col d'Izoard climbs northeast from the village of Guillestre through spectacular formations, pinnacles, and slopes not duplicated elsewhere in the Alps. It's a well-defined but obscure

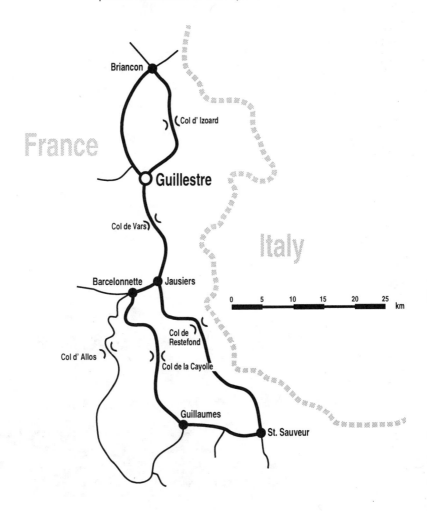

road that leads in 55 kilometers to **Briancon,** another fortress town.

Climbing southeasterly from Guillestre is the Col de Vars, leading in 50 kilometers to Barcelonnette. Just above Barcelonnette, at Jausiers, the Col du Restefond heads for Nice and the Riviera, only one pass, some gorges, and 130 kilometers away. The road squiggles up quickly to the pass, which may not be open until late summer, and then goes 50 kilometers south to the first intersection at St. Sauveur. Heading west from St. Sauveur over a couple of minor hump passes to Guillaumes leads to the south end of the Col de la Cayolle road. The Col de la Cayolle goes back north to Barcelonnette and Guillestre.

There are endless twisty roads and colorful gorges farther south, leading toward the Mediterranean, but that will have to be another book.

The Col de la Cayolle is just a few kilometers north and a couple thousand meters up from Nice and Monte Carlo on the sunny Mediterranean. The road was part of Napoleon's route from Elba.

South of
Andermatt

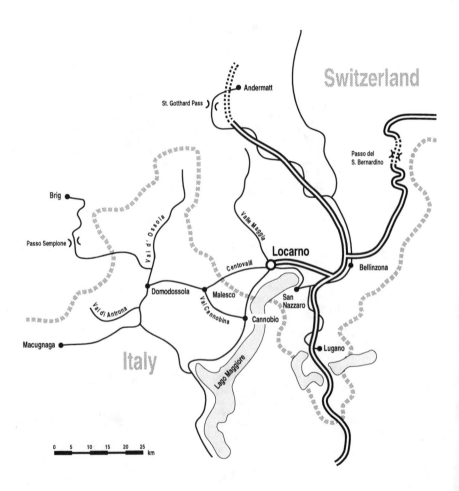

Lago Maggiore

If it gets a bit chilly or misty up in the high county, just do what the Swiss do: head for Lugano or Locarno, down in that Italian-speaking, pasta-eating part of Switzerland called Ticino. It's only an hour or two away. Hawaii, it's not. But around the lake shores there are real, if dwarf, palm trees, and oleander and hibiscus blooms—probably in pots—even while the snowy mountain peaks are still in sight. And there are some pretty good roads to get there on.

Locarno is on the north shore of a long, large lake called Maggiore. Part of the lake is in Italy, the rest in Switzerland. Lugano is on a smaller lake called Lugano, a bit southeast of Locarno. Why must the names sound so much alike? To confuse us.

Locarno, on Lago Maggiore, is small, sunny, and closer to the mountains than Lugano. It has hotels on the lake, on the hills, and in neighboring villages.

Right on the lake in Locarno is the **Beau-Rivage.** Rooms with a view of the lake are a bit more than "garden views;" Viale Verbano 31, or Box 43, CH-6600 Locarno-Muralto, phone 093/ 33 13 55, FAX 093/ 33 94 09. Just a few blocks uphill and down in price is a plain, practical hotel, **Hotel Carmine,** Via Sempione 10, phone 093/ 33 60 33, FAX 093/ 33 84 33. Across Lago Maggiore from Locarno, about 20 kilometers around the north tip of the lake, is **San Nazzaro,** where a modest hotel squeezed on the water's edge has great views across to Locarno and the Alps beyond from the dining room and some of the guest rooms; **Albergo Consolina,** CH-6575 San Nazzaro, phone 093/ 63 23 35 (the back rooms are close to a train track).

From the high Alps there are three pass roads leading down to Lago Maggiore: from Andermatt, the St. Gotthard Pass; from the Rhone Valley, the Simplon Pass; and from Graubunden and the Rhine Valley, the Passo del San Bernardino.

Trip 18 Passo San Gottardo

Distance	*About 100 kilometers from Andermatt to Locarno, one way*
Terrain	*Modern pass road and valley autostrada*
Highlights	*Quick way to get down out of the mountains, Passo San Gottardo (2108 meters)*

The St. Gotthard Pass from Andermatt (in Ticino, it's Passo San Gottardo) leads right down to Locarno. It's described in Trip 2, out of Andermatt. Once off the pass, it's autoroute all the way.

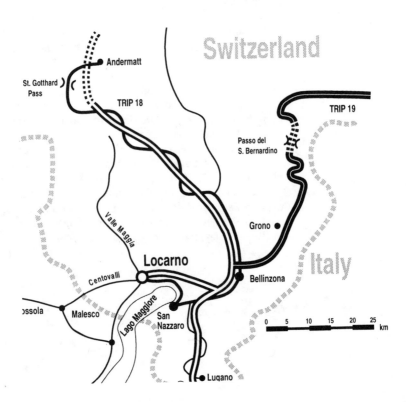

Trip 19 Passo del San Bernardino

. . . .

Distance   *About 105 kilometers from Chur, in the Rhine Valley, to Locarno, one way*

Terrain   *Tight, twisting, narrow mountain pass road, followed by high speed swooping across huge bridges to autostrada*

Highlights   *Rustic cafe on top of pass, exhilarating swoops, Passo del San Bernardino (2065 meters)*

From the Rhein (we spell it Rhine) valley in Graubunden, the San Bernardino Pass (in Ticino, Passo del San Bernardino) makes a direct and good ride connection to Locarno. The pass road is a sweeping, high-speed Autobahn most of the way from Chur in Graubunden in the Rhine Valley to Locarno. There's an all-weather tunnel under the highest peaks, but there's a twisty, attention-demanding road up over the pass, far above the tunnel, that's a motorcycle delight. A restaurant on a little lake at the top is a great refreshment stop, and a regular *Tofftreffpunkt*. Dine rustically upstairs if it's not comfortable sitting out.

The south side of the San Bernardino is on a magnificent series of sweepers with high arched bridges carrying the road back and forth over the valley below. In the lower valley is the village of **Grono** where Kiwi helmets are made.

Trip 20 Simplon Pass

Distance	*About 100 kilometers from Brig in the Rhone Valley to Locarno, one way*
Terrain	*High pass with high speed sweepers in (CH); Val Cannobina in Italy is narrow and tight*
Highlights	*Narrow and tight and fun, used by locals only, leads to lakefront road; Simplon Pass (2006 meters), a major pass between Italy and Switzerland; charming Centovalli and Val Cannobina, Swiss Army may be on maneuvers*

From the Rhone Valley, the Simplon Pass (Sempione in Italian) is in Switzerland all the way across, then enters Italy at its southern base. From here, there are a couple of fun connections back to Switzerland and Locarno: the Centovalli and Val Cannobina. Just after entering Italy at the base of the Sempione, before the Italian industrial town of Domodossola, the Centovalli road heads up and east toward Malesco. From Malesco, the road heads into Switzerland and down to Locarno. A pleasant route.

For a more challenging ride, head up and around Malesco's village church (not the big domed basilica on the edge of town which, incidentally, has a gruesome collection of pictures of vehicle accidents) and up over a narrow pass. Near a tunnel at the top, right on the edge of a lush, green, peaceful gorge, are some small memorial markers commemorating Italian partisans killed by the retreating Germans at the end of World War II. The road works down in a one-lane-wide collection of twisties through green forest to Lago Maggiore at an Italian town called Cannobio. From Cannobio it's a short ride north along the lakeshore to Switzerland and Locarno. (Lakeshore traffic can be tedious, and this little jaunt, however nice the views, may be all that's needed to illustrate the point.) Both the Centovalli and the Val Cannobina roads have rustic places to stop for refreshment.

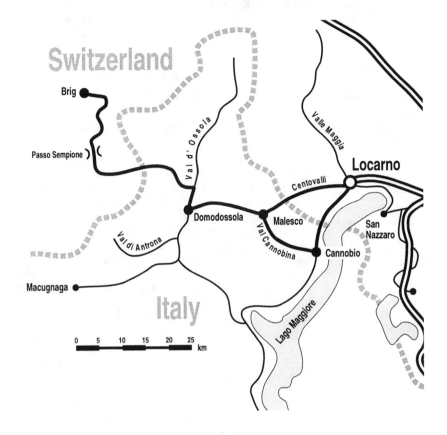

Trip 21 Valle Maggia

Distance	*Valle Maggia, about 120 kilometers round trip from Locarno; Macugnaga, about 160 kilometers round trip from Locarno*
Terrain	*Small, twisty roads into remote, high villages surrounded by giant mountains*
Highlights	*To explore where no one goes, try these dead end valleys*

A couple of kilometers out the Centovalli road from Locarno, it splits. The Valle Maggia road goes north and climbs through quiet villages with stone houses and roofs of huge stone slabs. The road narrows to work up switchbacks into high Alpine lakes where it dead ends, 50 kilometers from town. Nobody there.

Over toward the base of Passo Sempione, on the Italian side of the border above Domodossola, the Val d'Ossola climbs north almost to the Nufenen Pass in Switzerland. There's a *rifugio* near the lake at its top. (*Rifugios* are Italian institutions, usually staffed by a resident family to serve Alpine travelers and workers.)

South of Domodossola, at Villadossola, a wild little road climbs the Val di Antrona. There's a rifugio there, too.

A couple of kilometers south of Villadossola, a road climbs to a ski area known as Macugnaga, separated by Monte Rosa from Zermatt, Switzerland.

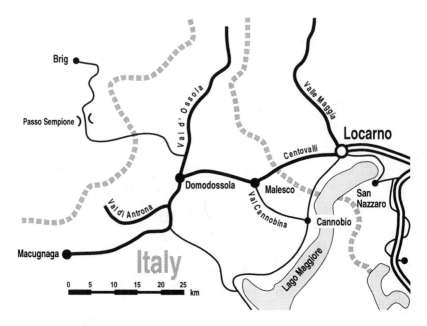

East of
Andermatt

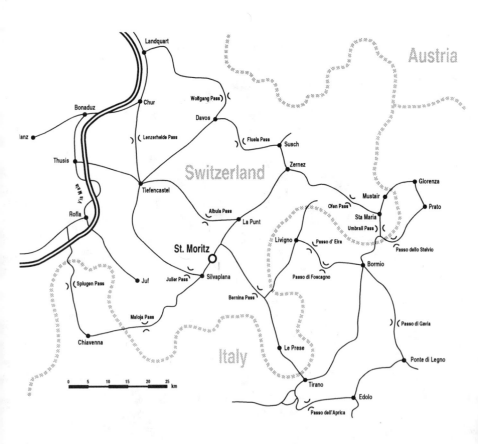

St. Moritz

East of Andermatt, over the Oberalp Pass, is the biggest and wildest of Swiss cantons, Graubunden, home of world-famous winter sports, St. Moritz, Davos, and more. Part of Graubunden is in the Rheintal (Rhein Valley) draining toward the North Sea, and part of it is in the Inntal, usually called Engadin, running toward Innsbruck, the Danube, and the Black Sea. A few parts in the south run into Italy and the Adriatic. Getting back and forth between these valleys across great mountain ranges makes for some good roads and good riding.

St. Moritz, in the high Engadin (valley of the Inn), is higher than a lot of passes, at 1822 meters. Even though it's high and cool and famous, St. Moritz and its neighboring resort villages are a logical base for exploring the great roads of Graubunden. Most facilities are available. Its reputation as the old-time playground of royalty means that there are old-time posh establishments, but there are plenty of places for ordinary bike riders. St. Moritz-Dorf (the German word for "village" is *Dorf*) is on the north slopes of the Engadin, up the mountainside from St. Moritz on the main valley road.

Right in the center of the Dorf, facing one of the few outdoor eating plazas (actually, one of the few level places in St. Moritz), is the **Hauser Hotel;** CH-7500 St. Moritz-Dorf, phone 082/ 3 44 02, FAX 082/ 3 10 29. Right behind the Hauser is the **Hotel Crystal;** CH-7500 St. Moritz-Dorf, phone 082/ 21 165, FAX 082/ 36 445. Both are modern and touristy, but right in the middle of the village.

Traffic through and near St. Moritz is encouraged to use the main valley road below the Dorf, but there is a good high road running east and west from the plaza at the Hauser Hotel.

For a real experience in how a Swiss hotel can coddle, and at about the cost of a modest hotel in the city, treat yourself to **Hotel Le Prese** in the village of Le Prese, south of St. Moritz, on the other side of the Bernina Pass, and almost completely surrounded by Italy. In an old building that has been modernized, the Hotel Le Prese is guaranteed to make everyone feel luxuriously cared for. There's a large outdoor pool. Almost all guests are annual regulars, with hardly a foreigner (non-Swiss) among them. Since there's a dress code, the management may discreetly arrange a dinner table with heavy linen and silver in the handsome bar room. Hotel Le Prese; CH-7749 Le Prese; phone 082/ 5 03 33, FAX 092/ 5 08 35. No credit cards.

Trip 22 Vorderrhein

Distance	*About 150 kilometers from Andermatt to St. Moritz, one way*
Terrain	*Narrow cliff-hanging road to major mountain highway*
Highlights	*Brief glimpse at a Switzerland no tourist sees*

The summit of the Oberalp Pass is just a few sweeping kilometers up from Andermatt. Then there's a pretty quick and tight descent as far as Disentis, followed by a long ride down the Vorderrhein valley (the "front Rhine") toward Chur, the capital of Graubunden, and the next good roads. Along the way, the Rhein goes through one of those "schluchts." The highway has to go up and around to the north of the Schlucht through the ski resorts of Laax and Flims. But there's a neat alternative. Chiseled out of the cliffs on the south side is a tight, narrow, cliff-hanging road known only to locals and exploring motorcyclists. It's easy to catch at **Ilanz** by crossing into the village from the highway and heading east, downstream, at the village square. The east end of the road is at Bonaduz, on the main routes to St. Moritz. From Bonaduz, the main road goes to Tiefencastel and then over the Julier Pass. (For more information about these roads, see Trip 23.)

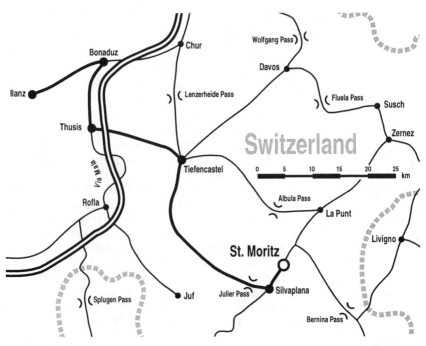

Trip 23 Hinterrhein

●●

Distance	*About 170 kilometers from St. Moritz, plus 50 to Juf*
Terrain	*Narrow, tight, steep climb, hairpins, and tunnels on Splugen; challenging, modern mountain highway on Maloja and Julier*
Highlights	*Audacious mountain road, awesome gorges, rustic rifugio, highest village in Switzerland, Maloja Pass (1815 meters), ★ ★ Splugen Pass (2113 meters), Juf and the Via Mala, ★ Julier Pass (2284 meters)*

Heading upstream (south) through the Engadin valley from St. Moritz, past some nice lakes, you don't feel like you're climbing. Then, suddenly, you come upon a real switchback downhill, the **Maloja Pass.** The Maloja heads down through some pleasant Swiss villages, one of which has such a narrow street that there's a traffic signal at each end to let vehicles pass one way at a time. The road heads over the Italian border. A bit into Italy, in the larger town of Chiavenna, there's a little traffic circle (watch for the brown sign, "Passo Spluga") and the beginning of a wild climb up the **Splugen Pass** back toward Switzerland. The pass road often just barely hangs on a cliff, often hairpins in a tunnel,

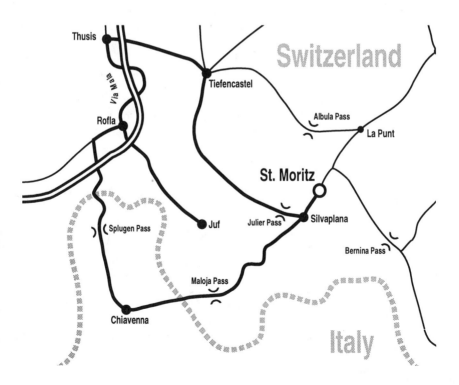

often works through stone snow shed tunnels that seem hardly helmet high and must have been built a century ago. Yet after snaking through stacks of cliff-hanging hairpins and one-way tunnels, in typical Italian fashion, the road ends in villages with people and trucks and buses, all using the road as their only connection to the world.

Short of the top of the pass, just below the face of a Mussolini-massive stone dam, is a typical Italian mountain rifugio, called **Rifugio Stuetta,** a fun place for a lunch, cappuccino, or good Italian hot chocolate. In a rustic wood-paneled room with a tiny bar, the host family will see that some kind of food, usually pasta and salad just waiting to be made, is available to refresh a weary traveler. It's a good place to remember that *bolognese* is meat sauce and *pomodoro* is tomato sauce, that oil and vinegar is the salad dressing of Italy, and that *formaggio,* cheese, will probably be Parmesan. Almost all remote Italian passes have these inns, staffed by a family in residence, which provide shelter and food to road workers and travelers. Invariably, there's one clean, though small, rest room.

Back in Switzerland, the road pulls one of the most amazing and oft-photographed series of ladder switchbacks in the Alps. The road goes back and forth so often on the alluvial mountain slope that you can pass by the same vehicles going in the opposite direction time after time.

Ten kilometers over the border into Switzerland, the pass road meets the high-speed San Bernardino Autobahn, a two-lane freeway. This is the valley of the Hinterrhein, the "back Rhine," to go with the Vorderrhein, the "front Rhine" leading down from the Oberalp.

Just ten kilometers down the Autobahn from the Splugen, an Autobahn Ausfahrt (exit) called Avers-Rofla leads to an adjoining Schlucht, and a Tofftreffpunkt at **Gasthof Roflaschlucht.** Opposite, a winding and deserted road leads south up to **Juf,** the highest permanent town in Switzerland, at 2126 meters. You'll find no tourists on this road.

Farther down the Autobahn, just before the Vorderrhein and Hinterrhein meet, is the Via Mala, the "bad way." The Autobahn sweeps through the gorge of the Via Mala in tunnels and bridges that make it easy to miss the narrow, deep gorge that for centuries was the "bad way." Take the Via Mala Ausfahrt and look down on what a frightening journey it must have been.

Below the Via Mala at Thusis, take the road toward Tiefencastel and the Julier Pass. The first part is another engineering tour de force, sweeping through an impossible gorge, playing back and forth at times with the Glacier Express train. **Tiefencastel,** wedged into a tiny valley, has gas, hotels, and a church typical of Romansch style: square stucco bell tower with an octagonal belfry topped by a dome.

The Julier road starts in Tiefencastel and climbs long, snaking up a gorge, then by a lake. Facilities at the top are good only for a postcard. Because the Engadin around St. Moritz is so high it's not far down to them from the top of the Julier into Silvaplana, a town with cute hotels and restaurants, and on into St. Moritz.

Almost all remote Italian passes have a rifugio staffed by a family in residence. This one, just short of the summit of the Splugen Pass, on the Italian side, is the Rifugio Stuetta. A welcome sight for the weary biker.

The north slope of Splugen Pass has an amazing series of switchbacks. This is September with a light covering of new snow that has been plowed. A few kilometers on, there's no snow.

Trip 24　Albula Pass

Distance	*About 190 kilometers from St. Moritz*
Terrain	*Three high passes and one medium high pass*
Highlights	*Cute Romansch villages, views of Glacier Express trestles, ski resorts,* ★ ★ *Moonscape on Albula Pass (2312 meters), Lenzerheide (1547 meters), Wolfgang Pass (1631 meters),* ★ *Fluela Pass (2383 meters)*

Right in the middle of a little village called La Punt, 12 kilometers down the Engadin (north) from St. Moritz, is the **Albula Pass** turnoff. It looks like a street of no significance between two buildings. The Albula is a back road. It climbs quickly above the tree line to the summit, and then bobs and weaves across a wild, rocky no-man's-land before starting down through lovely remote Romansch villages to Tiefencastel.

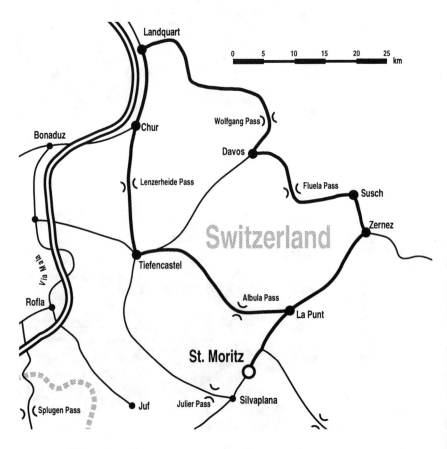

While the Julier Pass is considered the main auto road into St. Moritz, the train takes the Albula. Several of the bridges used by the Glacier Express along the route are famous on postcards and travelogues. Around the town of Bergun, the train makes several climbing loops inside the mountain, and below Filisur, the train crosses a gorge on a high stone arch viaduct, only to disappear at a right angle into the sheer granite cliff face.

The Albula leads down to Tiefencastel, quite a crossroads in its narrow gorge. This is where the Julier and Thusis roads meet the Albula Pass, plus a shortcut road toward Davos where the Fluela Pass starts, and the Lenzerheide road north over Lenzerheide. (For some reason Lenzerheide is never called a "pass," even though it's always listed as one.)

Lenzerheide is where the book *Heidi* is supposed to take place. It is very pretty country, but not exotic. The area centers around Chur, the canton capital, a large city with motorcycle shops and services, but the Lenzerheide road stays on the hillside above Chur and connects directly to the San Bernardino Autobahn. A 15-kilometer jaunt north on the Autobahn brings the rider to Landquart and the Wolfgang Pass road to Davos. Just short of the summit of the Wolfgang Pass is **Klosters,** where some members of the British royal family have been known to ski.

A couple of kilometers over the Wolfgang is **Davos,** with a one-way loop street that makes for an easy return to the Fluela Pass road. The Fluela, which has a pleasant, rustic restaurant at the top, crosses back to the Engadin below St. Moritz.

Once, 500 motorcyclists, on a rally sponsored by Michael Krauser, paraded though Davos past a reviewing stand with some notables, while the Davos town band played and replayed Queen Liliuokalani's "Aloha Oe," "Farewell to Hawaii."

Trip 25 Italian Connections

Distance	*About 230 kilometers*
Terrain	*Endless tight hairpins on Stelvio, second highest pass in the Alps; short unpaved section on Umbrail Pass; challenging modern pass road on Bernina Pass*
Highlights	*Good sweepers over ★ Bernina Pass (2328 meters) into Switzerland's farthest corner; a major motorcycle goal, the ★ ★ Passo dello Stelvio (Stilfser Joch; say "yoke") (2758 meters), with restaurant terraces, and hotels, vendors on top; Swiss national park, Umbrail Pass (2501 meters), Ofen Pass (2149 meters)*

The Bernina Pass, south from St. Moritz, swoops down and around, bypassing Pontresina, a popular resort. Then after climbing the first switchbacks, and just over some railroad tracks, there's a view point with the best views of **Piz Bernina** (the highest peak of the area) and its glaciers. The restaurants at the top are serviceable. Just across the top is an intersection

with a border crossing into the isolated Italian valley of Livigno (described below).

The sweeping southerly descent of the Bernina stays on good Swiss pavement. Below the town of Poschiavo is the little village of Le Prese, notable to bikers because of the train tracks that go down the middle of the street—well, almost the middle. It would be easier if they stayed in the middle. At the downhill end of the village, just as the tracks pull off to the side, is the **Le Prese Hotel.** Stop for lunch or refreshment on the lakefront terrace.

Recently an avalanche took out the road around the lake, below the hotel. Travelers had to take a boat across the lake until a precarious wooden ramp could be built. The ramp served until the permanent road could be rebuilt.

The Italian border is just a few kilometers on, with a steady parade of Italian cars crossing into Switzerland, tanking up on less expensive Swiss gas, and making a U-turn back to Italy. Not a bad idea.

Just into Italy is the Italian town of **Tirano,** where a turn north by the big yellow church starts the climb to the most famous motorcycle destination in the Alps, the **Passo dello Stelvio,** known in German as the Stilfser Joch. At 2758 meters, it may be the highest pass road in the Alps. Every motorcyclist has to climb it. The collection of stalls, shops, restaurants, hotels, and even a bank at the top of the Stelvio probably does violate environmental sense, but the convenience is unmatched.

Italy is building a two-lane freeway up the lower part of the valley from Tirano as far as Bormio, but the road over the pass above Bormio can only be described as *laissez faire* Italian determination. It seems like half the hairpins in the Alps are on the Stelvio, 40 or so on each side. And they are hairpins, with practically zero inside radius. Where there's room, the road may be almost two lanes wide, but much of the time, one narrow lane seems to strain the limits of the slope. In some places, the hand-laid rock retaining walls have obviously been pushed beyond their limits, and the road has slipped a bit down the mountainside. The Italian solution is to bridge the gap by pouring asphalt in the crack.

The Stelvio clearly illustrates the problem of mountain road building and maintenance. Surrounded by high cliffs, the alluvial slope is the only possible place to hang a road. And the alluvial slope is inherently unstable. The alternative, often used elsewhere in Italy, is a tunnel deep inside the mountain. But that surely spoils the view.

There's a road sign repeatedly seen in Italy: *lavoro in corso,* "work in progress." It perhaps should read "work needs to be in progress."

Whether it's sunny or foggy or snowy or rainy, there are always bikes on Stelvio. It's a must-stop for lunch or cappuccino or just tire-kicking. The postcard vendors know their market: there are plenty of cards showing the road, some with bikes in the hairpins. Skiers are permitted and there's summer skiing on the glaciers. There are even a couple of hotels on the top. **Hotel Stilfser Joch** (also known as Passo dello Stelvio Hotel); FAX 0342/ 903664. **Stelvio Hotel Perego** (recently remodeled); phone and FAX 0342/ 904553.

The northeast side of the Stelvio is equally exciting. It is often marked *chiuso,* "closed," but traffic is usually going around the barricade.

Just short of the top of the Stelvio, on the southwest (Bormio) side, is a border crossing back into Switzerland. This is the Umbrail Pass. From the border crossing it's all downhill. A reasonable portion of it is not paved, but is maintained in good condition. It goes down to the main Swiss road in the handsome Romansch village of Santa Maria, where the Ofen Pass climbs back toward the Engadin.

A fascinating alternate route to Santa Maria is to continue on across the Stelvio and, at the Italian base town of Prato, head north on a beautiful side road past the **Castle of Lichtenburg** to Glorenza (Glurns in German). From Glorenza, it's 20 kilometers to the Swiss border and the Ofen Pass road.

Just inside the Swiss border, above Glorenza, is the Swiss village of **Mustair.** Right on the road is a small church dating from the time of Charlemagne, famous for the earliest frescoes in Europe. Most of the frescoes tell the story of John the Baptist. The main ones focus on the gruesome aspects: tied up before Solome, then his head on the platter, etc., in the almost comic-book art style of the Middle Ages. The parking lot is across from the church, but bikes can usually park on the sidewalk by the gate.

Santa Maria has a good hotel just above where the Umbrail Pass comes down into town. It has good parking, restrooms, an outdoor terrace, and goulash soup. **Hotel Stelvio;** CH-7536 Santa Maria; phone 082/ 85358; FAX 082/ 85039.

The Ofen Pass, heading back toward the Engadin and St. Moritz, passes through the Swiss National Park. The park area seems very arid by Alpine standards, looking much like western parks in the U.S. From the Ofen Pass road, there's a one-way-at-a-time toll tunnel back into Italy and the Livigno valley. The small, narrow tunnel is several kilometers long. Traffic signals control the direction of traffic flow.

The last kilometers near the top of the Passo della Stelvio in Italy hang precariously on an alluvial slope. In this picture of the east side, the road has been outlined by an overnight snowfall.

There's always a crowd on the top of Passo della Stelvio. It isn't pretty, but it's exciting—sort of a motorcycle Mecca. There's skiing all summer on nearby glaciers so there are hotels and even a bank on the pass.

Trip 26 Duty-Free Livigno & Passo di Gavia

Distance About 230 kilometers

Terrain Rugged, high, challenging mountain roads

Highlights Passo d'Eira (2210 meters), Passo di Foscagno (2291 meters), Passo dell'Aprica (1176 meters), a high valley of Italy where everything is tax-free, including gasoline; also one of the Alps' more famous challenges, the ★ ★ Passo di Gavia (2621 meters)

Just over the Bernina Pass from St. Moritz is a border station, open during the day, into Italy. It opens to a nicely paved Italian Alpine road that leads to an Alpine curiosity, the duty-free high Alpine valley of **Livigno.** The valley is pretty well surrounded by Switzerland. The only Italian road out is up over two passes. Everything in Livigno is tax-free, including gas.

Free enterprise has not treated Livigno with gentleness. It's a hodgepodge. Most of what merchants think visitors should buy won't fit too well on a bike. Hotels and restaurants are adequate, but nothing special.

Besides the road from the Bernina Pass, there are two other ways out of Livigno. Straight down the valley, through the town and out the other side, a road winds around a lake to the toll tunnel back into the Swiss National Park.

The other way is through Italy, a bumpy 50-kilometer trip over two passes, the Passo d'Eira and the Passo di Foscagno,

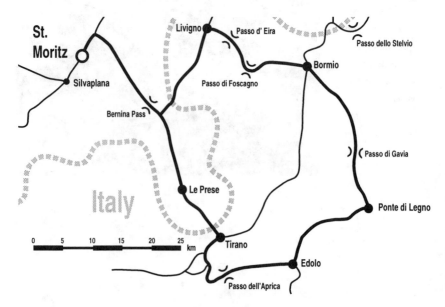

that few tourists or visiting motorcyclists see. The road ends at Bormio, the base of the Passo dello Stelvio and also the take-off point for Passo di Gavia, one of the higher roads in the Alps. Follow the brown signs for the Gavia in downtown Bormio.

From Bormio, the first 15 kilometers of the Gavia are standard highway. Then the fun begins. Much of the descent on the south side of the Gavia is narrow and unpaved, hanging on little ledges with rocky hairpins supported by flimsy old rock walls with hardly a piece of string or a tree branch for a guard rail.

This is another of those roads where "chiuso" (closed) probably means "travel at your own risk." Even when the road is closed, the rifugio at the top may be open, but there are no other services on the 35-kilometer crossing to Ponte di Legno.

Ponte di Legno is on a main east-west highway. Head west on the valley road to Edolo, where the Passo dell'Aprica road is straight ahead. The Aprica isn't high but has some ski hotels and restaurants right on the road through town. The west side of the Aprica has sweeping views of the Adda Valley which leads toward lake Como. But before that, about seven kilometers below Aprica, just after a tight curve that reverses the traverse, a little sign saying "Stazzona" points at a little road into the woods that works down the mountain to the main road toward Tirano. There, the big yellow church marks the gateway back to Switzerland, Le Prese, the Bernina Pass, and St. Moritz.

From a small border station on the Bernina Pass in Switzerland, a good Italian road leads into duty-free Livigno, an Italian valley almost surrounded by Switzerland, where everything, including gasoline, is tax-free.

Austria

Switzerland

Timmels Joch

Obergurgl

Jaufen Pass

Sterzing (Vipiteno)

Reschen Pass

St. Leonhard

Penser Joch

Certosa

Italy

Merano

Marling

Gampen Joch

Bolzano

Passo dello Stelvio

Fondo

Mendel Pass

Brennero Autostrada

0   5   10   15   20   25
km

Sud Tirol

Handsome is the word to describe **Merano,** Alto Adige, also known as Meran, Sud Tirol. Giant trees shade its streets. A mountain torrent regularly used for whitewater racing pours through its heart. Flowered promenades with coffee houses and *gelaterias* (ice cream parlors) follow the edge of the torrent. Its little medieval section has narrow arch-shaded streets lined with shops selling everything: bananas, nuts, pastries, leather goods, toys, the latest fashions. Behind the shops are beer gardens with the best Austrian and Italian food. Mountain peaks surround the town, lower slopes laden with apples and pears and vines. It's been the favorite spa of kaisers and kings. Yet Americans never stop in Merano. Say "Merano" to an American travel agent, and you will be corrected, "You mean Milano." No, Merano.

Merano is one of those places that has become Italian instead of Austrian only in this century. Much of the culture is both Austrian and Italian, and most everything has a name in both languages. You'll find pasta right beside Wienerschnitzel on many menus.

The mountainsides are lined with hotels. **Hotel Augusta** is a handsome yellow structure in a sort of Austrian Victorian style, secluded in a shaded garden just off the promenade. You'll find it at 2 Via Otto Huber, I-39012 Merano, Alto Adige; phone 0773/ 49570 (or Otto Huber Strasse 2, I-39012 Meran Sud Tirol); FAX 0473/ 49750.

Thirteen kilometers west of Merano in the direction of Reschen Pass and Stelvio, just past the village of Naturns, a great road called **Schnalstal** (Val Senales) climbs north toward the glaciers. The road's another alpine wonder. Several kilometers up the way, at Karthaus (Certosa), is **Hotel Schnalstal,** No. 60, I-39020 Karthaus; phone 0473/ 98102. Farther up the valley, at the top of the road, a cable car takes skiers up to summer skiing on the **Similaun Glacier,** the glacier where the multi-thousand-year-old ice man was recently found.

Up the mountain east of Merano is **Hafling,** famous for the small horses called Haflingers. From Hafling, a small road hangs on the mountain all the way south to Bolzano (in Bolzano, follow signs to Jenesien to reach Hafling).

Merano is a delight to be in, but it can be a pain to ride through. Brown signs do mark routes through town to the nearby passes.

Trip 27   Timmels Joch

Distance	*About 100 kilometers round trip to top of the pass*
Terrain	*Some congestion near Merano, narrow twisting climb, dark tunnel, on Italian side; more moderate on Austrian side*
Highlights	*Exhilarating views of glacieral peaks, connection to Austrian Tirol and Germany (toll),* ★ ★ *Timmels Joch (Passo del Rombo) (2509 meters)*

★ ★

The raging river through Merano is the Passer. Follow it upstream, north from Merano, 20 kilometers to St. Leonhard (San Leonardo in Italian), at the base of the Timmels Joch. On the way, the road passes the home of Andreas Hofer, a sort-of George Washington of the Sud-Tirol (only he didn't win). The house is now a Gasthaus.

The Timmels Joch is the lower leg of the fork in the road at St. Leonhard. It's a secondary road, narrow, tight, and twisty, hanging over deep canyons with a horizon studded with snowy peaks, and with some dark, rough-bottomed tunnels at the top.

Across the border at the top, on the Austrian side, there's a good restaurant. And the road quality improves—as well it should, because the Austrians collect a toll for traversing their side. It leads in a few kilometers to ski areas at Hochgurgl, Obergurgl, and Untergurgl, then continues into a long, pleasant Austrian valley.

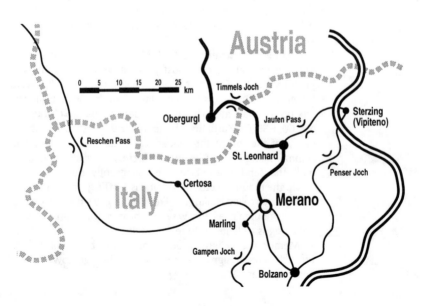

Trip 28 Reschen Pass

Distance	*About 160 kilometers round trip to top of pass*
Terrain	*Gentle climb on Italian side, a little more precipitous on Austrian side*
Highlights	*Orchards and farms, toll-free connection to Germany, leads to Stelvio, Reschen Pass (Passo Resia) (1504 meters)*

The main highway skirts around Merano on the west, and climbs a long valley toward the low Reschen Pass into Austria. On the way, it passes the turnoff for Schnalstal, the Stelvio Pass, and the turnoff for Santa Maria into Switzerland, and then some World War I forts and a ghost village sunk beneath the waters behind a dam with only the church steeple showing. Shaped like big igloos, the concrete forts were built by the Austrians to defend the pass from the Italians in World War I. Because the pass is low and has no toll, it's a favorite of Germans pulling trailers with low-powered sedans. It leads into the Engadin below St. Moritz and the Inn valley.

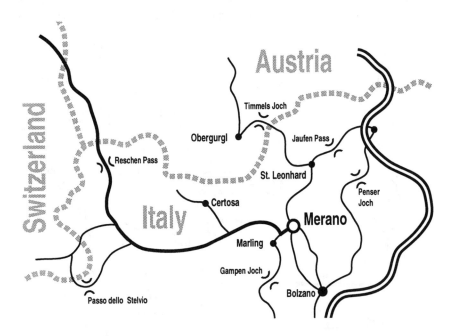

Trip 29 Merano

Distance	*About 170 kilometers*
Terrain	*Steep climbs and descents with hairpins, some narrow roads, over four high passes*
Highlights	*Neat farms, forests, properous villages, Tirolian culture, ★ Jaufen Pass (Passo di Monte Giovo) (2094 meters), ★ Penser Joch (Passo di Pennes) (2214 meters), Mendel Pass (Passo di Mendola) (1363 meters), Gampen Joch (Passo di Palade) (1518 meters)*

Starting at that fork in St. Leonhard, take the upper tine, the Jaufen Pass, a tight, narrow climb through forests, that burst above the tree line. There are only sandwich shops on the top. Then, a quick, steep descent into **Sterzing** (called Vipiteno in Italian). Sterzing is on the Brennero-Modena Autostrada, the major route between the cities of Italy and Germany.

Sterzing has an interesting but gotta-walk-in-to-see-it arcaded old street from the Middle Ages, similar to that in Merano, with many good restaurants. Try the four-cheese linguini. There's also a bike shop that deals in Moto Guzzi and choppers. On the wall is a photocopy of the cover of an American magazine featuring one of the local choppers.

The junction of the Jaufen Pass road with the Penser Joch road is outside Sterzing, so it's not necessary to go into the town unless you want to check it out. The Penser Joch road is marked

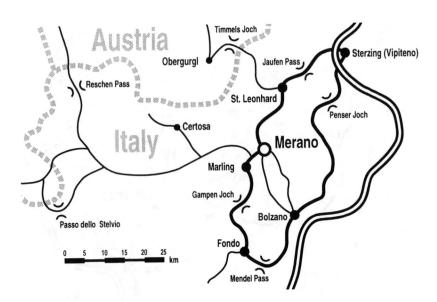

with one of those brown signs. It's a great twisting climb to the top, back up above the tree line, where there's an attractive rifugio restaurant. Then there's a long descent southerly, almost like a trip back in time, past flowering meadows and little villages and sturdy farmhouses. The valley, called **Sarental** (Val Sarentino in Italian), is completely Austrian in culture. Then some arched tunnels through a gorge and by a castle on a peak into Bolzano, a prosperous industrial city.

Bolzano (Bozen in German) is at the bottom of the deep canyon used by the Brennero-Modena Autostrada. It's just a couple of hours north to Munchen, and less than that south to Venezia. Bolzano has good motorcycle shops.

Keeping to the west through Bolzano, follow brown signs to Passo di Mendola (Mendel Pass), and regular signs to Eppan and Kaltern, towns on the way.

Mendel Pass climbs along cliffs with views of the deep canyon, the autostrada and railroad in it, and the river that made it, the Adige. Then it climbs into park-like green forests. A good picnic area. The culture is very Austrian.

Just over the pass where it's Italian again, turn toward Fondo, and from there onto the Gampen Joch road. The Gampen Joch (Passo Palade in Italian) climbs up, over, and down, with arched stone barriers on the edge of the pavement, typical of the Austrian Empire days. Toward Merano is the suburb Marling (Marlengo in Italian), with a good BMW dealer, well appreciated for having pick-your-own cherries, with one-pole ladders at the ready. Like many European BMW dealers, this one handles both cars and bikes.

Above the tree line on the Italian side of Timmels Joch, above St. Leonhard in the Sud Tirol, there are plenty of hairpins.

Riva and Lago di Garda

The south end of long Lake Garda, Lago di Garda (Italians are very casual about whether it's "del" or "di" Garda), is down in the flats of the Po Valley of Italy, near historic cities like Verona and Mantova. But the north end is up in the Alps, surrounded by giant vertical cliffs and snowy mountains. At the north point of the lake, surrounded by the cliffs of the Alps, is **Riva,** a small town and a beautiful destination.

Riva is a small lakeside resort, popular with Germans, and with all the amenities needed to serve the traveler—lots of shops, hotels, and restaurants stuffed inside some small fortifications of the Middle Ages. It is only 20 kilometers west of the Brennero-Modena Autostrada, and about 80 kilometers south of Bolzano, but a world away in spirit. It is signed from the autostrada at Rovereto, but it's a lot more fun to come down from the northwest, through Tione and over Passo Durone.

Coming from the Dolomites, follow the route that goes down and around Trento from Passo Manghen. On the loop

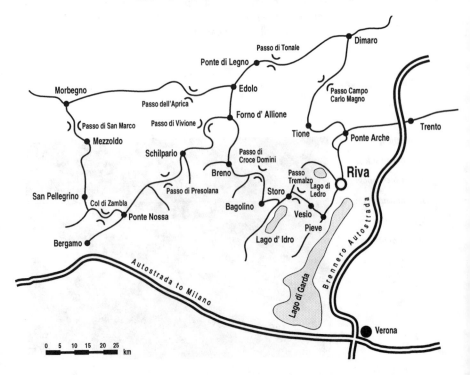

around Trento there are signs for Riva. Riva has a couple of motorcycle shops.

From Riva, there's a shoreline road around the lake that winds for miles through tunnels in the cliffs that rise a thousand feet or so out of the water. The road is in tunnels more than in daylight. Every driveway and intersecting road must be chiseled from the granite. Every spot where a wheel can fit has a restaurant or a hotel. One town, Campione, has a complete interchange tunneled into the adjoining mountain.

A road climbing west right out of Riva at the town's hydro-electric plant is literally a groove cut in the cliffs. Its function as a through road has been recently replaced by a long tunnel, but it provides great views of Riva—the "windsurfing capital of the world"—and the strange tilt-up strata beside the town that looks like a giant had played with it.

Lake steamers and hydrofoils come into Riva at a pedestrian square with lots of gelaterias. This is where elaborate concoctions are to be consumed leisurely, taking time to indulge in that great European sport, people watching. The sport is European, but Italians are the champions.

Traffic doesn't loop in Riva. It sort of gets shoved away from the lakefront on roads that don't seem to be going in the right direction. Keep an eye on those round, blue signs with white arrows showing which way it's legal to go.

Right on the pedestrian square is **Hotel Sole,** completely modernized on the inside, some rooms facing the lake; Hotel Sole, Piazza 3 Novembre 35, I-38066 Riva del Garda, phone 0464/ 552686, FAX 0464/ 552811. The piazza is not always open to vehicle traffic. Some fast talking and Italian arm waving might be called for to reach the hotel. Just don't hit a pedestrian. Next door on the lake is **Hotel Bellavista,** Piazza C. Battisti 4, I-38066 Riva del Garda, phone 0464/ 554271. Approach it by vehicle from the other side.

Riva sits at the north end of Lago di Garda, surrounded by high Alps and twisting roads. The road hugging the west shore of the lake is often in a tunnel chiseled through high cliffs that rise straight from the lake.

Trip 30 Pieve and Passo Tremalzo

Distance	*About 85 kilometers*
Terrain	*Gentle lakeshore with tunnels, steep, very narrow gorge, and dark tunnels; steep, rocky, unpaved section between Vesio and pass, smooth sweeping asphalt around Lago di Ledro*
Highlights	*Scenic lakeshore, exotic gorge and views from heights, rugged unpaved mountain climb, pass-top rifugio,* ★ ★ *Pieve and Passo Tremalzo (1894 meters) and Lago di Ledro*

Sited on the tip top of the 1,000-foot cliff, straight up over the lake with a balcony cantilevered into space, is **Hotel Paradiso** at Pieve. And the road to it is an absolute must. Follow the west shore road south about five kilometers past Limone, where the road suddenly opens up with no houses or businesses in sight. Take the 90-degree turn into a tunnel. The road climbs out of the tunnel, makes several hairpins, and goes in another long tunnel—parts of it in full width, parts in tight, narrow curves—to reach a narrow gorge with overhanging cliffs, dripping water, a grotto to the Madonna, and a little monument to Winston Churchill, who must have painted there. Honk the horn on one-lane blind corners. Traffic is two-way, but there's space for only one lane.

The road circles around at a little opening in the cliffs and crosses over itself. At that spot is a good restaurant specializing in trout—pick yours out of the tank.

In another couple of kilometers, at the top of the cliffs, is the village of Pieve. The uphill road from the traffic circle at the gas station climbs past the town piazza, church, and school, and there's the Hotel Paradiso, down a long drive to the cliff's edge. Swimming pool, tennis, and food.

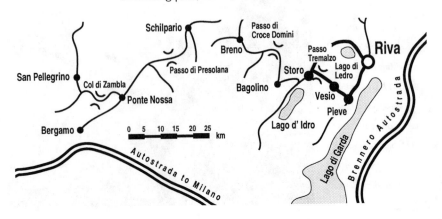

Once, a group of Americans at the Hotel Paradiso was supplied a menu in English. "What's this item, creamy noodle?" they asked. The hostess got out her Italian-English dictionary, which clearly translated "lasagna" into English as "creamy noodle." If you're lucky, they'll have "creamy noodle" as the first course.

If you stop just to look—and you should not miss it—buy something to eat or drink. Hotel Paradiso, I-25010 Pieve di Tremosine, Lago di Garda, Phone and FAX 0365/ 953012.

Passo Tremalzo from Pieve has become a dual-purpose legend since it was featured in *Motorrad,* the German motorcycle magazine. BMW has been seen testing new GS models in the area. The road up the pass is narrow, rocky, and unpaved, with hairpins hanging in space. A riding miscalculation could have very unsatisfactory results. It's not for uncertain riders, but all sorts of persistent street bikes have conquered it. Some may be happier going up it than down.

To find the pass from Pieve (not every intersection is marked), follow the signs from the gas station toward Vesio. The first several kilometers into a narrowing valley from Vesio are paved.

About halfway up, in a grove of trees, the pass road makes a hairpin into a fork going straight ahead, with some signs reading *vietato,* "forbidden." Whether or not it's forbidden, the straight-ahead fork isn't the right road.

At the top of the Tremalzo there's a good rifugio, and the other side, the north side, is all smooth, sweeping asphalt.

The asphalt descent from the rifugio ends on the Lago di Ledro road. It swoops around the lake of that name, and starts to descend the cliffs into Riva. That's where the old road's been replaced with a 90-degree sharp turn into the mountain and a tunnel several kilometers long into the back side of Riva.

The main road climbing the cliffs from Lago di Garda to Pieve is either hanging on a ledge or tunneling through a mountain. Honking is okay on blind, narrow corners.

Trip 31 The High Road West

Distance	*About 230 kilometers to Morbegno*
Terrain	*Three narrow, steep, paved, high mountain passes; and three less high*
Highlights	*Rushing streams and high mountain meadows with no traffic, rustic rifugios, ★ ★ Passo di Croce Domini (1943 meters), ★ Passo di Vivione (1828 meters), Passo di Presolana (1294 meters), Col di Zambla (1257 meters), ★ Passo di San Marco (1992 meters)*

A high route west from Riva uses remote passes known and used mostly by locals. Even those persistent explorers, German motorcyclists, seldom venture this way. This route crosses three high ridges between several roughly parallel valleys running south out of the Alps.

Cross the first ridge via the Lago di Ledro road out of Riva, going through the long tunnel, past the Passo Tremalzo turnoff, and across to Storo in the next valley.

From Storo, eight kilometers south on the valley road alongside a small lake, Lago d'Idro, the Passo di Croce Domini road intersects in a 170-degree right turn. After some heavy-duty climbing, you'll reach the mountain village of **Bagolino,** hung on steep slopes. It has a nice little piazza with a bakery/coffee shop. The outdoor tables have a view of the gorge and mountains, and the handsome colonnaded village church and campanile above.

From Bagolino, the Croce Domini road becomes one lane of dancing and climbing asphalt that runs beside torrents of water and rises out of the forests to cross the top above the tree line.

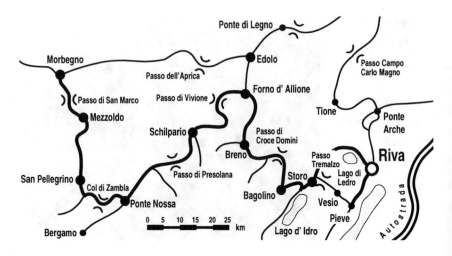

The rifugio at the top serves refreshments in front of, or practically inside, a giant fireplace.

The dirt road south from the Croce Domini rifugio is not recommended. The road down west from the rifugio has had problems with avalanches and slides, but has always been open to motorcycles. If the rifugio's family is absent, there are a couple of satisfactory mountain albergos just a couple of kilometers down the road.

Breno is a pretty big town at the westerly base of the Croce Domini. The valley north from Breno is surprisingly industrial (for a narrow Alpine valley), but it's only 20 kilometers to the Passo di Vivione, one of the most ignored delights of the Alps. Passo di Vivione starts westerly at Forno d'Allione. The pass road turns down across the valley stream, past a smelter furnace. Since *forno* means "kiln" and "furnace" as well as "oven," the turn is well named. In fact, the pass road is inconspicuous

A short distance from Riva is the tiny mountain village of Bagolino, with a tasty bakery and bar. It's a good stop before tackling the narrow, twisting heights of Passo di Croce Domini.

Passo Vivione is so devoid of traffic that it's easy to conclude there's nobody else on the road.

around and beyond the parking lot of the smelter. The whole pass is one-lane, paved, and devoid of traffic.

The little ristorante just across from the smelter is delightful At this ristorante, the cook is also a wood carver, delighted to show off both his skills. Take note that in all of Italy, the large noon meal, usually more than a lunch, is over by 2:00 p.m. and the kitchen is closed.

Because the pass has so little traffic, it's easy to assume that all of the one lane is usable to play on. But there can be other vehicles.

There's a rifugio at the top of the pass, usually run by a little old man. From it are views of empty valleys and jagged mountain peaks.

The pass comes down on the southwest to Schilpario, a ski resort. Below Schilpario, resist the temptation to turn down into the deep valley. Rather, stay on the higher road which leads right up Passo di Presolana, in the direction of Bergamo. The road passes through a resort area popular with Italians, but unknown to most foreigners. There are several good hotels and ristorantes in towns like Rovetta and Clusone, but no English is spoken.

Five kilometers below Clusone, just below the village of Ponte Nossa, the Col di Zambla road climbs west, while the valley road continues to the large city of Bergamo. (Bergamo was home to Montessori.) The Col di Zambla road comes down in the next valley by **Terme San Pellegrino.** Terme means spa or "bad." This is the San Pellegrino of bottled water, often rated the best of bottled waters (better than Perrier?). The bottles and their plastic carriers and the trucks hauling it all will be in evidence. The spa itself looks well past its prime. The International Six-Day Trials were once held in the area.

Passo di San Marco is a rarity: no other bikes. It's not marked. Follow the valley north from San Pellegrino, taking the forks toward the town of Mezzoldo (some maps erroneously show the pass from the area of a town called Cusio, but that's the wrong valley). The high road from Mezzoldo is the pass. It crosses over and comes down into the town of Morbegno in Adda Valley (the valley that could be seen from Passo dell'Aprica, upstream from Lago di Como). From Morbegno, there are good connections into Switzerland via the Splugen Pass and the Bernina Pass. (See Trip 23, Maloja Pass, Splugen Pass, etc., and Trip 25, Italian Connections.)

Trip 32 The Low Road West

Distance	*About 210 kilometers to Morbegno*
Terrain	*Three modest passes; occasional hairpins and grades, mostly main roads*
Highlights	*Faster route west than Trip 31, more interesting than autostrada in Po Valley; Passo Campo Carlo Magno (Madonna di Campiglio) (1682 meters), Passo Tonale (1883 meters), Passo dell'Aprica (1176 meters)*

Taking the higher road north from Riva to Ponte Arche and over to Tione leads to the north-south **Passo Campo Carlo Magno** and the ski area **Madonna di Campiglio,** both in the woods, under the tree line.

At Dimaro, the pass road intersects with the westbound road over Passo Tonale, a barren pass with a World War I *sacrario* (cemetery). The Tonale road comes down to Ponte di Legno (the base of Passo di Gavia in Trip 26), and from there to Edolo and over Passo dell'Aprica toward Switzerland at the Bernina (see Trip 25).

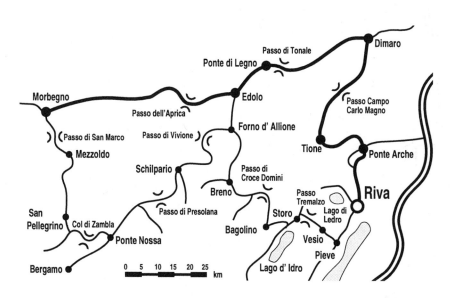

The Dolomites

The Italians call them Dolomiti, and the Germans, Dolomiten. Whatever they're called, the first view of the Dolomites will take your breath away. No matter how many mountains you've seen, no matter how many times you may have seen the Dolomites, that first glimpse—maybe as you emerge from a tunnel, or maybe as you accelerate out of a hairpin—will be an almost religious experience. The vertical massifs set in feathery green forests are duplicated nowhere. And there are more good roads than a good rider can cover in a week of hard riding.

Draw a straight line on the map between Venezia (Venice) and Munchen (Munich). There in Italy, just below the middle of that line, are the Dolomites. They're east of that giant canyon known as the Brenner Pass, the great divide made by the Adige River which is used as the major and lowest north-south route across the Alps.

There are good low-level routes around the Dolomites, so no one has to go through them to get anywhere. The only people there are there because of them. The Dolomites are a skier's and motorcyclist's dream.

The Dolomites are in Italy, with Italian laws, stamps, and money, but it was not always thus. Until World War I, they were in Austria, part of the Tirol. The Austrians were on the Germans' side in World War I, and the Italians were on the Allied side. The Austrian and Italian generals ordered up battles much like the horrible ones in France, only these were in the mountains. Little known in our history books are the costly battles fought between Austria and Italy in the Dolomites. Once one side or the other had charged up or down a mountain at great loss of life, they had to build a road to supply the dearly bought area. They built roads and tunnels that didn't seem to go anywhere except to serve some strategic need of the moment.

Now those roads make up a fantastic network for motorcycle exploring. Besides the roads, the war left only *sacrarios* (cemeteries) and some huge stone forts.

History doesn't indicate that the costly battles in the Dolomites decided anything, but at Versailles the victorious allies awarded the Sud Tirol (South Tyrol) to Italy. In the 1920s, some of the Tirol voted to return to Austria. The rest, including the great Dolomite range, is now known in Italy as the Alto Adige.

Vast areas of the region still remain Germanic. Many towns have Austrian-style buildings and food and are known by their German names. Typically, one side of a pass, usually the south and east side, will be completely Italian, while the next village, just a pass away, will be Austrian-Germanic. A quick clue: besides the pictures painted on the sides of the buildings, Austrian villages will have a church with a steeple, while an Italian town will have a church with a campanile.

Whether the village is Italian or Austrian, it'll have fresh pasta and great cappuccino. The Austrian ones will have Wienerschnitzel as well. A hotel or restaurant in either will have a dining room set with fresh linen and glasses, and another with bare tables. A meal may be available only in the room with the tablecloths, but there will always be a cover charge for sitting there. Noon time is siesta time and full meal time in Italy, and pasta is just the first or second course. (If pasta and salad is enough for lunch, make that clear, or the courses will keep coming.)

Cortina d'Ampezzo, usually known simply as "Cortina," is the most famous village in the Dolomites. It's spectacularly set on the eastern edge of the Dolomites and has been the site of winter Olympics. Regularly reviewed in travel magazines, it's the summer resort of choice for the wealthy of Milano. (It's a lot cooler than Milano.) Cortina's central pedestrian zone has pricey shops, and a department store with everything, called the Cooperativa. *The New York Times* once said something to the effect that the place to be seen is the bar of Hotel della Post in Cortina. Motorcyclists have been seen there, and also watching the scene from the narrow terrace in front of the hotel. It's a treat to have a drink, especially if the owner, S. Manijgo, is around to talk about the history of the valley. His family has owned the hotel for more than a century, and he has the photos to prove it. Cortina is nice, but expensive.

There's a figure eight loop, lying on its side, in the heart of the Dolomites just west of Cortina. The trip includes six major passes. Just as in Andermatt in Switzerland, it's possible to ride the figure eight and expand into the almost endless variations beyond it without ever coming down into lowlands or big cities.

Each of the villages on the trip has hotels and restaurants, many nicer, and all cheaper, than those in Cortina d'Ampezzo. The middle of the figure eight is Passo di Campolongo, only ten kilometers across. The towns at each end of the pass have good accommodations.

The south anchor of Passo Campolongo is **Arabba,** a completely Italian town with good food and a variety of comfortable hotels. Tourist Information; I-32020 Arabba; phone 436/ 79130; FAX 436/ 79130.

Spacious rooms and a parking garage can be found at **Hotel Evaldo,** one of the several hotels in Arabba. It has a sauna and jacuzzi and makes a point of serving motorcyclists. I-32020 Arabba; phone 436/ 79109; FAX 436/ 79358. Very friendly, but not much English spoken. Demi-pension dinners at the Evaldo include pasta (say tagliatelli or cannelloni), or aubergine (eggplant), or soup as the first course, then entrecote (steak) or veal, vegetables, salad bar, and dessert.

Ten kilometers north across Passo Campolongo, at Corvara in Badia (usually called just "Corvara"), things are a bit more Germanic. A variety of hotels includes **Hotel Posta-Zirm,** an old-time place that's been modernized and has grown in all directions to include a lovely dining room, an indoor pool, and a ski lift at the side door. I-39033 Corvara, Phone 471/ 836175; FAX 471/ 836580. Dinners include an elaborate salad bar at the Zirm, a good place to mix the American custom of eating salad before the main course with the European one of having it afterwards. Breakfasts are bountiful by Euro standards.

An option in Corvara would be a handsome new albergo overlooking the village and surrounding massifs: **The Gasthof Alisander,** Phone 471/ 836055; FAX 471/ 836686. (*Gasthof* is usually translated into Italian as *albergo*).

The New York Times says to stay in **La Villa** (*Wengen* in German), a village north of Corvara.

This best of all views of Cortina d'Ampezzo, a major resort of the Dolomites, is from the Belvedere at Pocol, a little village on the Passo Falzarego, where it intersects with Passo Giau. See Trip 34.

Trip 33 Dolomite Figure 8

Distance	*About 90 kilometers*
Terrain	*Climbs and descends with lots of hairpins and switchbacks; some cobblestones*
Highlights	*Six major passes encircle fantastic vertical massifs; many cafes and hotels. Includes: Passo di Valparola (2192 meters), Passo di Falzarego (2105 meters), Passo di Campolongo (1875 meters), Passo di Gardena (Grodner Joch) (2121 meters), Passo di Sella (2244 meters), Passo di Pordoi (2239 meters)*

Passo di Valparola starts just downstream (north) of Corvara about five kilometers, at a village called La Villa in Italian and Stern in German. The handy signs for the passes are in distinctive brown color. Towns are in blue. The road goes southeasterly across a stream and climbs though several ski resorts. Near the top is the ruin of a massive World War I fort, set amidst a moonscape of Dolomite rocks and crags. A few kilometers north of the summit, the south end of the pass stops at the summit of Passo di Falzarego. To the east, the Falzarego descends in hairpins past magnificent vertical formations toward Cortina. The figure eight goes the other way, westerly, in a series of hairpins and tunnels. But not too far down. It hangs high on the edge of the mountain back toward Arabba, villages and fields a thousand meters below on one side, snow capped massifs on the other, a thousand meters up.

The southern legs of the figure eight, the Passo di Falzarego and the Passo di Pordoi, make up part of the Great Dolomite Road which goes east from the Brenner road to Cortina. This is

124

the most touristy part of the Dolomites and the oldest pavement. Still, it's so exciting as to be a must. An occasional tour bus may require every inch of the road to get around a hairpin. Remember, when tempted to duck past a bus, that the rear wheels will track inside of the front. In the Alps when the going gets tight, the descending vehicle is supposed to back up. Tourists are early risers, and are usually off the roads by 4 p.m. The roads and colors are good through the long summer evenings.

Each of the passes on the figure eight has tourist facilities. There are several cable cars to the peaks.

At Arabba, the Falzarego joins the Passo di Campolongo heading north, and the Passo di Pordoi, still the Great Dolomite Road, climbing west. Passo di Pordoi has 33 numbered hairpins on the east side out of Arabba, and 27 down the west side.

Before the west base of the Passo di Pordoi at Canazei, the Passo di Sella starts heading north on the figure eight. All of the massifs are famous for mountain climbing, but the Sella is probably the best known. Usually there will be climbers hundreds of meters overhead and hikers with binoculars watching them from below.

The Sella comes down a bit on the north, only to intersect the Passo di Gardena heading east on the figure eight. The passes intersect at a road heading west to the Brenner through the **Val Gardena,** a valley very popular with German tourists, who call it Grodnertal. The valley is loaded with Germanic hotels, and shops selling copper and leather goods.

The Passo di Gardena's east end is downtown Corvara, where one fork in the Y intersection is the Passo di Campolongo climbing south to Arabba, ten kilometers away.

No matter how many mountains you've seen, the first glimpse of the Dolomites takes your breath away. It's almost a religious experience. This first view is from Wurz Joch, a pass that climbs out of the great canyon of the Adige river.

One of the 27 hairpins on the west side of Passo Pordoi, part of the Great Dolomite Road.

The north side of the Passo Campolongo, part of the "Figure Eight" loop in the Dolomites. These mountains are shaped like no others.

The top of Passo di Giau in the Dolomites has a serviceable rifugio and gorgeous views.

Trip 34   Dolomites: Marmolada

• •

Distance	*About 50 kilometers from Canazei to Pocol*
Terrain	*Steep mountain roads with hairpins*
Highlights	*Almost as fantastic as Trip 33, plus a narrow gorge, all with a lot less traffic. Includes: The Marmolada (Passo di Fedaia) (2057 meters), and Passo di Giau (say JOW, rhymes with "how") (2233 meters)*

★ ★

These passes are east-west connections south of the Great Dolomite Road. They're all Italian, from Canazei at the bottom of the Pordoi on the west, to Pocol on the east, just above Cortina on the Falzarego.

Starting east from Canazei, the Passo di Fedaia is off the normal tourist route. It climbs the flank of the Marmolada, the largest massif of the Dolomites and the site of some of the bloodiest fighting of World War I. There's a lake at the top of the Fedaia and a ristorante across the dam on the south side of the lake, with views of the massif.

At the tree line on the east side of the Fedaia, the old road descends through a narrow spectacular gorge, only one lane and one vehicle wide. Overhanging rocks obscure the sky. A new highway, built around the gorge, tunnels through the mountain and daylights onto a bridge that crosses the gorge at right angles, only to disappear back into a tunnel on the other side. The view from the bridge is good. The view in the tunnels isn't.

To get onto the gorge road coming down from the pass, go to the right side of some buildings at a ski lift, just as the road veers left. The gorge road looks like it might be a parking lot on

the right side of the buildings. Entering the gorge from the bottom, go straight ahead on the narrow cobble road in Palue to Sottoguda, where the main road goes left and starts climbing. If the road into the gorge is marked *chiuso* (closed), remember that in Italy (only in Italy), "closed" usually means "travel at your own risk."

The Italians have experimented with making the road through the Sottoguda gorge one way. Because it's so narrow, it is probably wise to conform to whatever the current signs suggest. If necessary, take the new main road to the other end. It's worth the time and trouble.

The area is noted for hand wrought iron work. Some interesting, some weird creations are displayed on buildings in the valley.

Below the gorge is a village called Caprile, way down in a deep valley. From Caprile, start climbing up the wonders of the Passo di Giau by following the signs to Selva di Cadore. Just before Selva, the Giau pass road has a well-marked turn up the mountain. There are a couple of rugged rifugios on Giau offering basic food and shelter, good for a warm drink or an overnight escape.

Going into Selva instead of turning up the Giau leads you to Passo Filla Staulanza (1773 meters) and either Passo Duran (1601 meters) or Passo di Cibiana (1530 meters). From either, main valley roads lead back to the figure eight. The east side of the Giau has some delightful picnic spots.

The Giau comes out on the Falzarego pass road just above Cortina at a small village called **Pocol.** Here is one of the most impressive World War I monuments and mausoleums in the Alps, and the best view of Cortina. Neither the monument nor the view are visible from the road, and they are not well-marked. To find them, turn up a little driveway just below a big old hotel, usually closed. There's a little sign, "*Sacrario.*" It's just a hundred meters up the drive to the monument entry gates. They may have an international "do not enter" sign, but the keepers have usually let motorcyclists with respectful attitudes ride in. The monument itself is a church, with the stations of the cross set on each side of a stair cut through the mountain leading to it. The cut frames the monument against the Cortina valley.

The best view of Cortina is from a *Belvedere* (a terrace with a view) just a few meters past the gate to the monument.

On the east side of Passo Fedaia, motorcyclists want to take the old road through the Sottoguda gorge, not the new road that only gets a brief view of the gorge from the bridge above. The rest of the new road is in tunnels.

Trip 35   Southern Dolomites

Distance	*About 130 kilometers from Arabba (add another 100 to San Baldo)*
Terrain	*Paved mountain roads, some steep tight turns*
Highlights	*Feathery forests, dramatic vertical mountains, little traffic, several rifigios. Includes: Passo Filla Staulanza (1773 meters), Passo Duran (1601 meters), Passo Cibiana (1530 meters), Passo di Valles (2033 meters), Passo di San Pellegrino (1918 meters), Passo di San Baldo (703 meters), Passo di Rolle (1955 meters), Passo di Cereda (1378 meters), Passo di Brocon (1616 meters)*

A 15-kilometer jaunt south, down the valley south from Caprile, away from the figure eight, leads to Cencenighe, the gateway to Passo di Valles and Passo di San Pellegrino. Both go west.

Passo di Valles has a comfortable rifugio at the top with good lasagna. The western slope of Passo di Valles is velvety green. It looks like a park, and it is. Both passes descend deep into the Valle di Fassa, the west extension of the Great Dolomite Road.

The westerly end of the Passo di Valles road is at a T intersection with the Passo di Rolle road. Head north at the T to go back to the Great Dolomite Road. Or head south, up and over Passo di Rolle to Fiera, where a northwest turn leads over Passo di Cereda. Passo di Cereda has two humps, the lower of which is called Filla Aurine. From the north end of the Cereda,

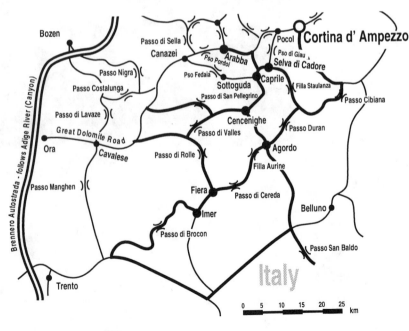

130

it's possible to head back to the figure eight through Agordo or to continue on over more passes. Passo Duran climbs up to 1601 meters. From the north end of Duran, it's possible to head back toward the figure eight via the Passo Filla Staulanza, or continue on in the direction of Cortina via the Passo di Cibiana. These passes offer Dolomite type views and usually have little traffic.

To explore farther or to head toward Trento, go south five kilometers from Fiera on the Passo di Rolle road to Imer. At Imer, take a road up and west to Passo di Brocon, where a rifugio awaits you at the top.

These passes mark the southern edge of the Dolomites. There are some good twisties farther south, and one more pass worth a detour because of the audacity of its construction. Called Passo di San Baldo, it crosses a ridge at only 706 meters, not high enough to note otherwise. It's about 15 kilometers southwest of Belluno, one of the major cities south of Cortina, and was the high water mark of the Austrian advance during World War I. The Austrians got down over the ridge in one place, but there was no supply road. So they had to build one. This road is carved out of the cliff face back and forth. But there was no room for a hairpin at the end of each traverse. So the road goes into the mountain in a tunnel, makes a hairpin, and comes out going the other direction. Then it does the same thing in reverse. The hairpin tunnels are stacked five or six deep, one on top of the other, at each end. They are not lighted!

Once, pulling into Pocol at the east end of Passo di Giau, a rider at the side of the road was studying a map. He was on a Munch, that massive, in-line, four-cylinder machine made in Germany before the Japanese made such a layout their own. "Hey, wait while I get a picture of you and the bike." "Sure, but if you wait a minute there will be a hundred Munchs." And there were.

Way down south is a pass of amazing audacity: Passo di San Baldo. Each end of each traverse is a hairpin in a tunnel! The tunnels are stacked five or six deep.

Trip 36 Adige Canyon

Distance	From Arabba via Wurz Joch, about 60 kilometers to Brixen; via Passo Nigra, about 60 kilometers to Bozen; via Passo di Lavaze and Passo Manghen, about 140 kilometers to Trento
Terrain	Often narrow, occasionally challenging pass roads. Wurz Joch and Passo Manghen have practically no traffic.
Highlights	A sense of exploring on traffic-free routes to the Brennero Autostrada; ★ Wurz Joch (2002 meters) and Passo Manghen (2047 meters) have attractive rifugios. Includes: the Brenner Pass, the canyon of the Adige River, Passo di Costalunga (Karer Pass) (1745 meters), Passo Nigra (Niger Pass) (1688 meters), Passo di Lavaze (1805 meters).

On the great Dolomite passes, even the bottoms of the passes are high. Cortina at the east end is over 1200 meters, and Canazei at the west end is over 1400, so there's still a lot of mountain riding to get to the bottom of things. The great divide, the canyon of the Adige River, home to the Brennero Autostrada, is close to bottom at about 250 meters.

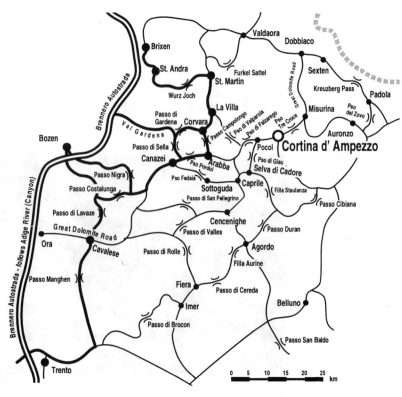

Once down on the Brennero Autostrada, it's only a couple of hours to Munchen, Venezia, Padua, or Milano. Like all Italian autostradas, the Brennero is a toll road, so entrances and exits are few. Upon entering, push a button for a ticket which is then used to compute the toll upon exiting. The autostrada is a handy way to make time going north or south. Entrances northbound are marked "Brennero" and southbound entrances are marked "Modena." (Modena is a city way down south across the Po Valley.)

The Great Dolomite Road finally gets down to the Adige River and the autostrada at Ora, after a bunch of tunnels and hairpins often full of trucks, buses, bicycles, and pedestrians.

Many alternate roads go up over mountain passes on the way to the Adige, and all of them finally find a tributary gorge to follow down. Better to take one of the up and over and down routes than the Great Dolomite Road.

The most beautiful and most fun motorcycle road between the Great Dolomites and the Adige Canyon is the Wurz Joch, known in Italian as Passo di Erbe. Find it downstream (north) from Corvara, about 15 kilometers north of La Villa and the figure eight. The sign points west to a village across the valley called St. Martin, but there should be a brown sign for Wurz Joch (Passo di Erbe). Above St. Martin, the pass road goes right around a private little castle.

The pass reaches the Brennero Autostrada in three humps. Wurz Joch is the highest. The road is good as far as the top of the Wurz Joch, where there's an attractive rifugio called **Utia de Borz.** The deck is a great place to contemplate a first or last view of the Dolomites. West from there, the road is one lane through woods and meadows. Hardly anybody there. When the road splits, follow signs to St. Andra, and then on to Milan. There are several attractive hotels around St. Andra, where the road takes up two lanes again.

The pass road gets to the Brennero Autostrada at **Brixen,** a handsome city with shaded streets, squares, and a famous restaurant called **Elefant.** Seems some eastern potentate of the Middle Ages was shipping a prize elephant to the German emperor across the Brenner Pass. The elephant expired in Brixen. The restaurant named after the unfortunate beast is attractive and has many dining rooms, all different and interesting, some with balconies. The menu is huge, eating there an adventure.

Going east toward the Dolomites from Brixen, the Wurz Joch is not marked. Follow signs to Milan, a neighboring village, and then to St. Andra. From St. Andra the one-lane road seemingly going downhill is the Wurz Joch road.

Another major access routes into the Dolomites from the Brennero Autostrada is the Val Gardena. Unlike the Wurz Joch, the Val Gardena route is well marked from the autostrada. It leads through a popular resort area known to the Germanics as St. Ulrich, and to the Italians as Ortisei. The area is full of hotels. The Val Gardena road ties into the figure eight trip between the Passo Sella and the Passo di Gardena. About 11 kilometers west of Canazei is the turnoff for the Passo di Costalunga road. Then, just past the top of the Costalunga, the Passo Nigra goes up again, north and west. Both continue down to the Adige Canyon at **Bozen** (Bolzano) on the Brennero Autostrada. Bozen has all services expected of a major city, including traffic. It's home to Iveco trucks and buses.

Finding the Costalunga and/or the Passo Nigra from the bottom at Bozen requires careful attention. Both take off just north of the city from the old highway that leads to the Brennero Autostrada. There's no connection or marking from the autostrada. The signs are easy to miss among the traffic and commercial activity of the highway, even though the highway seems to be hugging the edge of high cliffs. It's worth the effort, though, because either of two roads will provide both instant relief from the congestion and some fun riding. The crowds will not be going this way.

Passo di Lavaze is a north-south mountain connection roughly parallel to the Brenner Pass. It starts up and south from the Passo di Costalunga road at a country intersection downstream from the village of Nova Levante (labeled Welschnofen in German). Signs point to Nova Ponente (Deutschnofen). At the top of Passo di Lavaze, an unpaved pass called Passo di Occlini (Grimm Joch) goes westerly. Lavaze is anchored on the south by the town Cavalese on the Great Dolomite Road. Just cross the Great Dolomite Road for a further north-south mountain connection, Passo Manghen. Go down into the valley below Cavalese where the Passo Manghen road heads up a finger canyon. It's about 20 kilometers to the top.

Most experienced Dolomite hands don't know of Passo Manghen, even though it has great riding. It's all one lane wide, but two-way traffic, with tight switchbacks in dark forests. It just makes it out above the tree line. On the south slopes there's a rustic but attractive rifugio called **Bar Trattoria Molga-Voltrighetta.** The south end of the Manghen is on another main valley road that heads down west to Trento (Trent in German and English), a major city in the Adige Canyon and the Brennero Autostrada.

This main valley road to Trento descends and goes around Trento without going into it, crossing the Brennero Autostrada. Then there's signing for Riva del Garda that seems to be going in the wrong direction, but works. The signed route to Riva climbs a new road west out of the Adige valley. The nicest route into Riva is to head west to Ponte Arche and then south.

During World War I, the Austrians defended the top of the Passo Campolongo from the Italians with a massive stone fort, all in a never never land of jagged peaks and boulders. (See Trip 33.)

There are some lovely picnic spots in the Dolomites, for example this one on the east side of Passo Giau. (See Trip 34.)

Trip 37 Cortina

Distance	About 40 kilometers to Drei Zinnen; about 120 over Kreuzberg and back
Terrain	Irregular sweeping mountain pass roads
Highlights	Mind-boggling views from Drei Zinnen (toll); forests, vertical massifs, restaurants and hotels. The trip includes: Passo Tre Croce (1805 meters), ★ Misurina and Drei Zinnen (Tre Cime di Lavaredo) (2320 meters), Passo del Zovo (1476 meters), Passo di Monte Croce (Kreuzberg Pass) (1636 meters), Furkel Joch (1759 meters)

Like many European cities, Cortina has a one-way loop street system. Some of the core inside the loop is pedestrian zone. If you miss a stop or turn, the only solution is to go around again. Cortina's loop isn't round—there are some switchbacks and some hairpins—but by the third or fourth circuit, it becomes familiar. In the course of circling Cortina, you'll see brown signs pointing the way to the Passo di Falzarego and to Passo Tre Croce. Both start climbing right in the village, the Falzarego westerly, and the Tre Croce easterly.

The Tre Croce is pleasant enough. The prize is **Lake Misurina** just east of the pass. Its exquisite blue reflects the surrounding Dolomite massifs. There is a bit of entrepreneurial clutter. On the north side of Lake Misurina, still just minutes out of Cortina, a little road marked "Drei Zinnen" and/or "Tre Cime" takes off to the east. It's a dead end, private toll road that

climbs up several hundred meters in a series of hairpins and sweepers that reveal dramatic views of Dolomite crags, the very best view of the Dolomites possible with wheels still on the ground. The cameras will be out.

From Misurina north, it's all downhill to Dobbiaco (Toblach) and the main roads into Austria.

The roads farther east are not Dolomite dramatic. At Auronzo it's possible to go back behind the big domed church and get out of the valley traffic on the Passo del Zovo. It heads north and connects with the Kreuzberg Pass in the direction of Austria.

The Kreuzberg Pass (Passo di Monte Croce in Italian) has nice hotels and good views of the Dolomites. **Hotel Kreuzberg Pass** has many facilities including an indoor pool. I-39030 Sexten-Hochpustertal; phone 474/ 70328; FAX 474/ 70383. The turn off for the Kreuzberg from Austria is at Sexten (Sesto in Italian).

North of Corvara, a little-known pass called Furkel Sattel cuts across some pleasant mountains. Its chief interest is that it cuts out a bunch of congested valley traffic and makes a direct connection with Staller Sattel (see Trip 38), one of the best ways into or out of Austria. From the road north of Corvara, five kilometers downstream from the turnoff to the Wurz Joch at St. Martin, is the village Longega, squeezed in the gorge. That's where the Furkel Sattel road heads up a finger valley. Then at St. Viglio, the pass road goes north. The road straight ahead through St. Viglio dead ends, but the Furkel Sattel passes some minor ski resorts and some lovely vistas over Tiroler countryside, then comes out on the north at the village Valdaora (Olang in German) on the main road into Austria, and at the south end of the Staller Sattel.

Trip 38 Three Passes to Austria

Distance	About 70 kilometers from Cortina to Austria at Staller Sattel; about 150 kilometers to Austria at Plocken Pass; about 175 to Austria at Nassfeld Pass
Terrain	Exciting climbs by forests and lakes
Highlights	Green lake, one-lane road on ★ Staller Sattel (2052 meters); populated valley roads wind to Plocken and Nassfeld Pass (1557 meters). Interesting switchbacks on Plocken Pass (1362 meters)

North of Cortina and about ten kilometers east of Brunico (Bruneck) at Valdaora (Olang), the Staller Sattel takes off toward Austria. The intersection is right beside a lumber yard. The pass road winds through lovely Tiroler fields, past a glacier blue-green lake, and climbs to the pass in a fun-and-games, one-way road through the forest. The one-way part is controlled, so there's 15 minutes for up traffic and 15 for down, with 15 minutes to clear each way. So there's only 15 minutes an hour to start up or down. The border guards are at the top to make sure there's no cheating.

About 14 kilometers down into Austria, just below the village of St. Jakob (one of those villages where the road jogs

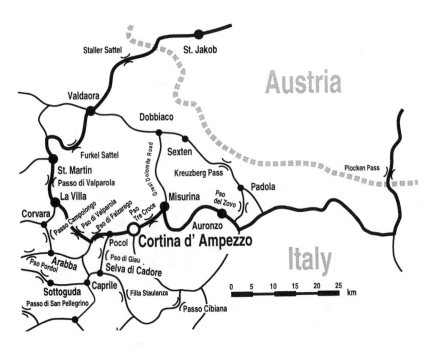

around an old house), there's a beautiful hotel restaurant right beside the road called **Tandlerstub'n;** A-9963 St. Jakob. A great place to try Schweinshax'n, a Bavarian and Austrian specialty. The best translation is "hog knuckles" and that falls far short of describing the succulent slices of pork here. The "joint" will be dramatically served on a huge platter with all kinds of trimmings including Semmelknodel, a kind of dumpling.

Two other passes farther east are useful as escapes from valley highway traffic:

About 75 kilometers east of Misurina, through moderately interesting countryside and the town of Sappada, the Plocken Pass makes a dramatic climb into Austria. (There is an unpaved pass just south of Sappada, Filla Lavardet.) The Plocken Pass (Passo di Monte Croce Carnico in Italian) isn't high, but the switchbacks are dramatic. It's a good gateway to the south end of the Grossglockner (see below).

Another 30 kilometers farther east, the Nassfeld Pass road climbs quickly into Austria from the autostrada at Pontebba.

Traffic is permitted only one way at a time on the west side of Staller Sattel, so these bikers can

safely plot the line of their choice, using the whole road.

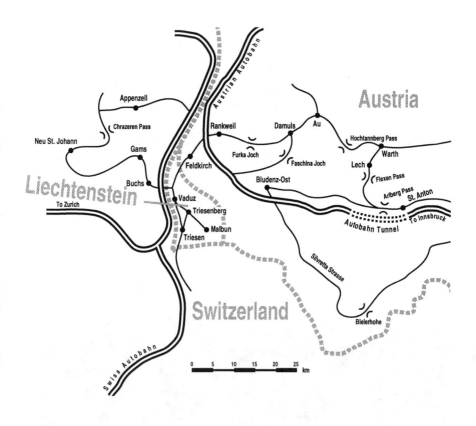

Liechtenstein

Liechtenstein is that little, rich country where the prince lives in the castle on the hill and every once in a while they have a skier in the Olympics. About 30 kilometers long and 15 wide, it's sort of in the Alps, using Swiss money, German language, but its own stamps. Switzerland is to the south and west; Austria is to the north and east. The Rhein, flowing north now, marks much of the boundary with Switzerland. This is downstream from the Vorderrhein and the Hinterrhein and the Via Mala and Chur (see Trips 22, 23, 24). Just across the Rhein is the Swiss Autobahn. You can get anywhere from Liechtenstein.

Vaduz, the capital, and several other villages in Liechtenstein are pleased to accommodate motorcyclists as well as sell stamps.

From the castle-topped village in the south called Balzers, an interesting road runs through the woods, over a little pass, and through a stone military gate into Switzerland and the cute Swiss village called Maienfeld, leading to Landquart and Wolfgang Pass (see Trip 24).

In the middle of the country, starting at Vaduz or the village of Triesen, a Liechtenstein mountain road climbs to the villages of **Triesenberg** and **Malbun.** Triesenberg hangs high on the mountainside and has gorgeous views of the valley of the Rhein and Schwagalp. Malbun, on through a tunnel from Triesenberg, is in a high ski bowl at about 1600 meters.

The secret way up to Triesenberg and Malbun is the narrow, cliff-hanging, one-way (up only) road that starts at the prince's castle.

At Triesenberg a good hotel is the **Martha Buhler** (named after the skier), FL-9497 Triesenberg, Liechtenstein; phone 075/ 2 57 77, FAX 075/ 8 15 20. Farther up is **Rizlina Berg Gasthaus,** hung on the edge of the mountain. Same address. Phone 075/ 2 02 24.

One of many hotels in Malbun is the **Montana,** FL-9497 Malbun, Liechtenstein; phone 075/ 2 63 7322; FAX 075/ 8 22 72.

Liechtenstein's Tourist Office is FL-9490 Vaduz; phone 075/ 2 14 43; FAX 075/ 2 08 06.

About that (FL)? Furst is a German word for prince. So the Principality of Liechtenstein becomes Furstentum Liechtenstein.

Trip 39 Liechtenstein

· ·

Distance   *About 60 kilometers explores the whole country*
Terrain   *A few narrow, one-way roads, some sweeping climbs, a slippery tunnel*
Highlights *Good views of the Rhein Valley, castles, hotels, restaurants*

By the time you've found the places mentioned in the introduction, you will have seen all of Liechtenstein.

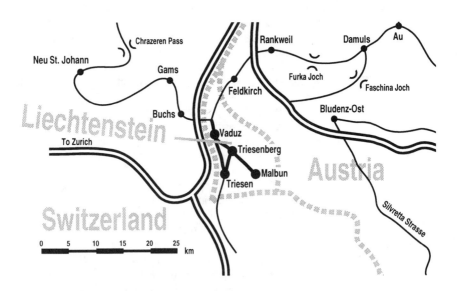

Trip 40 Santis and Schwagalp

Distance	*About 100 kilometers round trip from Liechtenstein*
Terrain	*Gently climbing and sweeping mountain roads*
Highlights	*Less-traveled Switzerland, Chrazeren Pass (1278 meters)*

A loop climbs through the lower Swiss Alps just across the Rhein from Liechtenstein into the remote little canton of Appenzell. Appenzell has been most famous recently for its method of voting in public meetings, from which voting, women have historically been excluded. Still, it's sort of romantically quaint, with buildings and people that look the way Swiss buildings and people should.

Across the Rhein from Liechtenstein, past the sizable Swiss town of Buchs, at the village of Gams, a road climbs west across the south side of Santis mountain. This road with little traffic crosses a minor pass of about 1000 meters at Wildhaus, and comes in about 25 kilometers to the village Neu St. Johann. There, a mountain road heads east toward Appenzell over Chrazeren Pass. This is no Furka nor Susten Pass, but a forest and meadow road, with some imposing granite peaks around. At the top of the pass, a turnoff leads to the base station of a cable car that goes up the mountain, Santis. For some reason, the parking lot and restaurant at the cable car is a *Tofftreffpunkt*. The road goes on down to Urnasch, then to the town of Appenzell, where a small road heads back toward the Rhein Valley.

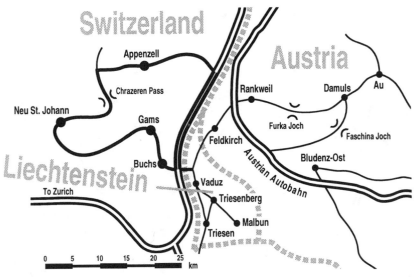

Trip 41 Western Austria

Distance	*About 260 kilometers*
Terrain	*Some sweeping, some twisting climbs and descents; narrow road on Furka Joch*
Highlights	*Lovely farms, forests, glacier views at ★ Silvretta (2036 meters), hotels, restaurants, ski resorts. Includes: Arlberg Pass (1793 meters), Flexen Pass (1773 meters), Hochtannberg Pass (1679 meters), Faschina Joch (1487 meters), Furka Joch (1761 meters)*

Austria knows how to take care of tourists. Practically every corner has an attractive Gasthaus or hotel, with "Zimmer freis" in between. *Zimmer frei* means "room available," and is the Germanic equivalent of "bed and breakfast." Invariably, they're good and reasonably priced.

The most western state of Austria, called Vorarlberg, and its capital, Feldkirch, are right at Liechtenstein, but separated by high Alps from the rest of the country. So it takes some pretty good pass roads to tie Austria together. Since most Alpine pass roads run north-south, these Austrian roads going mostly east-west can be entertaining as well as useful.

The main one is the Arlberg Pass, now with an Autobahn and a tunnel to take the trucks and buses off the good mountain road. It starts at Feldkirch, which is really on the north border of

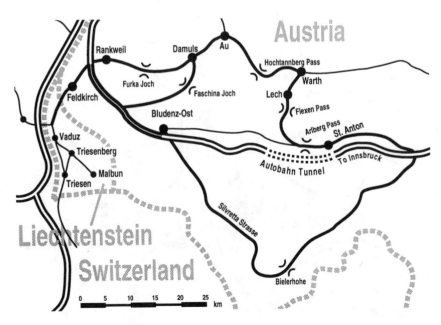

Liechtenstein. Might as well take the Autobahn from Feldkirch as far as Bludenz-Ost. (Don't confuse Bludenz on the Arlberg road with Bregenz, north of Feldkirch on the Bodensee, site of popular summer music festivals.)

At Bludenz-Ost, one of the best roads in Austria heads south. Called the Silvretta Strasse, it roughly parallels the Arlberg, but takes a rollicking time getting there, so it has only enthusiasts on it. And, welcome to Austria, there's a toll. Austria has a lot of toll roads.

After a short run up a valley past sturdy Austrian farm houses and neatly manicured pastures, the road has an exciting steep climb with switchbacks and hairpins and views of the same, up to a lake. This is a *Stausee,* a good German word meaning a lake created by a dam. Then there's more climb to a higher lake and the pass, Bielerhohe, where there's a delightful restaurant terrace with views over the lake reflecting snowy peaks.

A refreshing non-alcoholic drink available nowhere but Austria and Bayern (Bavaria) is Spezi (spait zee). It's an orange flavored cola. A big one, a "grosse Spezi," usually comes in a half-liter beer glass.

From the top, the pass road works down eastward to a pleasant valley where it connects again with the Arlberg road. Just before the junction, there's a good view of a castle and an often photographed high bridge called **Trisannabrucke** that carries the railroad up the Arlberg.

Heading west, back up the Arlberg from the junction, the old road is a good climb that also avoids the toll tunnel under the pass. Watch for the beautiful Austrian farm houses showing considerable pride of ownership. With elaborate corner bay windows, deep arched doors, balconies, and wide, overhanging roofs, they are often decorated with pictures and maybe poems or historical names in Gothic script. Contemporary ones are of block construction with light beige stucco and dark brown trim. The gable end almost always faces the road. On a pole over the front gable end is a lantern-like bell tower. Some of the lanterns are pretty ornate.

The old road up the pass is okay because the traffic is taking the Autobahn tunnel. Along it are a bunch of saintly towns: St. Jakob, St. Anton, St. Christoph, all of them labeled "am Arlberg" to distinguish them from towns of the same name scattered all over Austria.

Just west of its summit, the Arlberg intersects the Flexen Pass. The Flexen heads north in a series of fairly tight sweeps covered by wooden snow sheds hung on the mountain. Just over its top are the famous ski resorts of **Zurs** and **Lech,** in the valley of the Lech river (Lechtal) and the Austrian state of Tirol. Both towns have noteworthy buildings decorated with pictures of saints and local heroes, or maybe the building's first owner. The Hotel Post in Lech is particularly nice. (Every town in the

Alps has a Hotel Post.) Lech has attractive outdoor restaurant facilities. If tablecloths are out, the place is in operation.

Seven kilometers below Lech, at Warth, there's a hotel on the corner popular with bikers, where the Hochtannberg Pass heads west.

It's about 23 kilometers westerly over the Hochtannberg to the village of Au, where the Furka Joch road heads back to Rankweil and Feldkirch. (This is Furka *Joch.* Furka *Pass* is at Andermatt, Switzerland, and Furkel Sattel is in the Dolomites.) Above Au, at a village called Damuls, a new road heads back to Feldkirch over a pass called Faschina Joch, 1487 meters. Furka Joch, a remote, nobody-takes-it-on-purpose road, goes on through Damuls.

Damuls has a couple of nice hotels. One, the Adler, has a good baker as well as cook. **Hotel Adler,** A-6884 Damuls, Bregenzerwald; phone 055/ 10220-0; FAX 055/ 10220-10.

Heading the other way, looking for the Furka Joch from Feldkirch, follow the signs first to Rankweil.

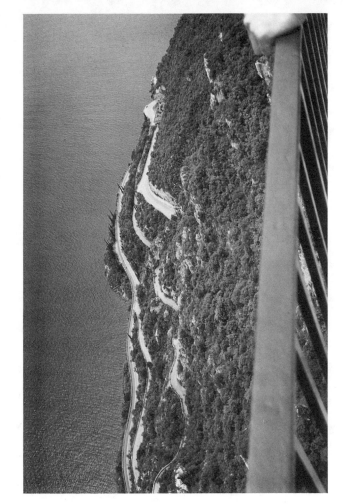

Looking straight down at Lago di Garda from the balcony of the Hotel Paradiso shows the lower reaches of the road climbing up from the lake. (See Trip 30.)

Austrian Tirol

Innsbruck is the historic capital of the Tirol, site of Olympics, and a good-sized city that's no fun to drive in or through. Strategically located where the Brenner Pass to Italy reaches the Inntal (valley), it's hard to miss. The mountains are so close around that there are no immediate alternative roads. The Autobahn in the Inntal goes by Innsbruck hung on the edge of the mountains. It's free and it's the recommended route around Innsbruck. Innsbruck looks nice from the Autobahn. The Brenner Autobahn from Italy makes a T with the one in the Inntal at Innsbruck, but it's a toll road.

The Inn River comes down from St. Moritz in Switzerland (see Trips 22–26) and heads easterly through Innsbruck, where there is indeed a *brucke,* a bridge, and finally north to Germany where it flows into what we call the Danube (in German, it's Donau). The Autobahn follows the Inn around to Germany, so while Munchen lies straight north of Innsbruck, the Autobahn connection loops around to the east. The Autobahn remains the fastest way to get to Munchen.

To add to the general geographic confusion, the only Autobahn route from the Tirol in Austria to Salzburg and Wien (Vienna), both also in Austria, goes into and through Germany.

For tourist information about Innsbruck and the immediate area, contact the Tourist Office; A-6021 Innsbruck; Austria; phone 0512/ 59 8 50; FAX 0512/ 59 8 50 7. Imst is a town about 70 kilometers west of Innsbruck in the Inntal, where several good pass roads come together. A possible hotel in Imst is the **Post;** A-6460 Imst; Austria; phone 054/ 12 25 54; FAX 054/ 12 25 19 55.

All the roads in Tirol are easily available from Ober Bayern (southern Bavaria).

Trip 42 Innsbruck Passes

Distance   *Via Brenner Pass, about 30 kilometers to Italy; via Timmels Joch, about 100 kilometers to Italy; via Reschen Pass, about 100 kilometers to Italy; about 100 kilometers via Piller Hohe up Kaunertal*

Terrain   *Brenner: low pass, major Autobahn; Timmels Joch: long, sweeping valley to high exotic pass; Reschen: long valley run, low pass; Kaunertal: steep mountain climb*

Highlights   *Brenner Pass: quick route to Italy (toll), fantastic bridges; Timmels Joch (2483 meters): nice valley villages, sweeping climb to high mountains (toll); Reschen Pass: no toll, leads to Passo della Stelvio; Piller Hohe (1558), Kaunertal (2750 meters), Timmels Joch, Reschen Pass (1504 meters)*

It's a short, quick run, less than 50 kilometers, over the Brenner Pass from Innsbruck to the area of the Italian passes around Merano (see Trips 27–29) and the Dolomites (Trips 33–38). That's the Brenner's chief merit. But it's so low and so congested that it hardly deserves other comment.

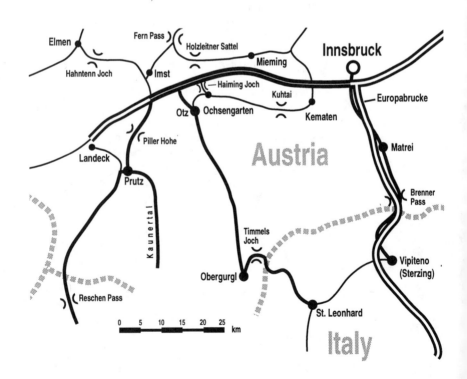

There is a *Bundesstrasse,* a non-freeway, non-toll, federal road, across the Brenner alongside the Autobahn. It has usually been the choice of motorcyclists. From it, the gigantic structures of the Autobahn, including the famous **Europabrucke bridge,** look awesome. But the road goes through a picturesque town called Matrei am Brenner with one narrow street that has tried to outlaw motorcycles. Various courts are hearing various appeals of the arbitrary decision. The only way around Matrei is the toll Autobahn.

If there's time, it's more fun to take the ★ ★ Timmels Joch rather than the Brenner Pass, or even the Reschen Pass. The Timmels Joch (its other end is described in Trip 27) parallels the Brenner starting about 45 kilometers west of Innsbruck, near Kuhtai and Haiming (see Trip 43).

The Reschen Pass (see Trip 28) starts up out of the Inntal at Landeck, about 75 kilometers west of Innsbruck. It's mundane, lower, and a bit more of a detour than the Timmels Joch. A good way to get to the Reschen is to head south, up and out of the Inntal from Imst, short of Landeck, over a little-known pass, Piller Hohe, and come out on the Reschen Pass at Fliess or Prutz. Little Piller Hohe allows the rider to sail along the high mountain, occasionally looking down on the traffic in the Inntal. From Prutz a road up the dead end Kaunertal valley leads to a *Stausee* and one of the highest roads in Austria. The upper part has a toll.

Trip 43   Obscure Tiroler Roads

Distance	*About 250 kilometers*
Terrain	*Some sweeping, some tight narrow mountain roads*
Highlights	*Famous castles, churches, little-used mountain roads, nice restaurants and hotels. Includes: Ammer Sattel (1118 meters), Berwang (1336 meters), ★ Hahntenn Joch (1903 meters), Haiming Joch (1685 meters), ★ Kuhtai (2017 meters), Seefeld in Tirol; Telfs; Holzleitner Sattel (1126 meters), Fern Pass (1209 meters)*

In Ober Bayern (southern Bavaria), the mountains and roads are exciting when compared to the Great Plains, but the real riding is readily available in the high Alps of the Austrian Tirol just across the border. This trip is easily accessible from Munchen as well as Oberammergau and Garmisch, and anywhere in the Tirol.

Starting from the town of **Ettal,** just outside Oberammergau and just north of Garmisch, escape the traffic and tourists by turning south over the Ammer Sattel. Ettal has a huge domed baroque monastery church right near the intersection. Apparently the monks make good brandy, and the handsome gold and white interior of the church has consumed some of the profits.

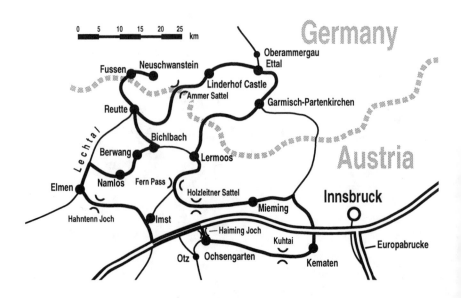

The turn is marked with signs for the **Konigschloss Linderhof,** one of Mad King Ludwig's castles which is ten kilometers up the road. The German noun *Schloss* is almost always translated to the English word "castle." This can be misleading, because Schloss can also mean "palace." (No walls or battlements on a palace; a castle may have a moat and other fortifications.) This Konigschloss, royal castle, is Ludwig's small baroque jewel of a palace, with a jet fountain and an underground lake for Wagnerian opera, built in the late 19th century. It can't be seen from the road. Tours take a couple of hours.

Ludwig was king of Bayern in the days that Bismarck was uniting Germany under a German, rather than an Austrian Kaiser. Ludwig's sympathies were with the Austrians, which as it turned out, was unfortunate. Meantime, he built two other castles besides Linderhof to play in: **Neuschwanstein** is the turreted wonder on every travel poster, near Fussen and Reutte; and **Herrenchiem See**, on an island in a lake named Chiem See, between Munchen and Salzburg. Of course, he had inherited other castles and palaces. Neuschwanstein was the inspiration for Disney's Magic Kingdom castle. Herrenchiem See on the island is supposed to look like the French Chateau of Versailles.

Past Linderhof, the Ammer Sattel road goes through a forest and climbs to the low *Sattel* which happens to be the Austrian border. Into Austria a few kilometers, the road winds around an Alpine lake called Plansee, with a nice hotel at the end of the lake closest to the border and several serviceable restaurants. Then it makes a rather windy, steep descent into Reutte (say "Roy tuh"), a bustling Tiroler town.

Reutte has a two-lane Autobahn around it which can seem confusing. Follow signs south toward Lermoos and Fern Pass, away from Germany (D), and exit in a couple of kilometers at Bichlbach and head for Berwang and Namlos. This is delightful rural Tirol. Some of the road is barely one lane, dancing around high Alpine meadows. Berwang has nice-looking hotels.

The road comes down in the *Lechtal* (the valley mentioned in Trip 41). Five kilometers west up the *Lechtal* at Elmen is the obscure turnoff for a great, usually ignored pass, the Hahntenn Joch. The narrow road crosses a little field and then starts climbing the rock face in a long steep traverse before turning into a high valley for some more twisting fun. There are no facilities at the top, which has a huge slope of sliding alluvial granite, but short of the top is a cute Gasthaus named **Zur Gemutlichkeit;** A-6644 Bschlabs 31, Lechtal, Tirol; phone 056/ 35 259, FAX 056/ 35 521. (How many other towns start with five consonants?) It faces an equally cute onion-domed church.

The narrow road comes down through woods into Imst, another prosperous Tiroler town with a typical Austrian church.

Bavarian churches typically have onion domes on the tower. Austrian churches, like that at Imst, have a square tower with a clock face on each side, then an open belfry topped with four gables finished off with a tall pointed steeple.

Imst, like Reutte, has a sort of two-lane bypass Autobahn around it, connecting with the major east-west Autobahn in the Inntal between the Arlberg and Innsbruck.

Head toward Innsbruck about ten kilometers to a small village named Haiming on the north side of the highway. Opposite the village, heading south up the mountainside, is the Haiming Joch road. It's hardly more than a driveway. The signing is to Ochsengarten. This narrow, one-lane road climbs past steep fields, with little haystacks and occasional Zimmer Frei signs and a Gasthaus with a view of the whole valley, into a high forest, and then comes down just a bit to the Kuhtai road at the intersection called Ochsengarten.

Kuhtai is a high pass, but for some reason it's never called a pass, just Kuhtai. It goes east-west, roughly parallel to the Arlberg-Innsbruck Autobahn down in the Inntal, but higher in the Alps. Even though it's close to such traveled ways and to Innsbruck, it never has traffic. At Ochsengarten, it seems hardly more prominent than the tiny Haiming Joch road.

West from Ochsengarten, the Kuhtai road makes a steep descent to Otz, on the Timmels Joch road. Kuhtai, the pass, is the other way, east and up over the tree line past a massive earth dam and its lake. There are a couple of ski hotels at the top. Then a fairly modern road sweeps down east in a long valley called the Sellraintal. Some straights end in rather abrupt tight corners. After several cute villages, the road enters a tight gorge shared with a raging mountain torrent. Then, without further ado, it ends in the Inntal, at a village named Kematen, just a couple of kilometers from downtown Innsbruck.

Here, the secret is to go straight ahead through Kematen and under the Autobahn, and sweep up the mountain on the north side of the Inntal. This is the main *Bundesstrasse* (federal road) toward Garmisch in Germany. But up the mountainside a few kilometers, still in Austria, is the exit for Seefeld. Seefeld is famous for cross-country skiing. Guess that means it's flat on top. West of Seefeld, a delightful little road hung on the mountainside heads for the Tiroler town of Telfs. Straight on through Telfs toward Holzleitner Sattel, the road passes through **Mieming,** known to many motorcycle tour-takers as the home of Edelweiss Bike Travel.

The west side of the Holzleitner has wonderful, wide sweepers down to the picturesque village of Nassereith. But first, on the way down, pause to view the lush green Tiroler valley below. Often there's a vendor selling *heiss Wurst und Brot,* the Tiroler equivalent of a hot dog, only better. A good munch helps you contemplate the view.

North from Nassereith is the Fern Pass, a nice road, with too much traffic and too many anxious drivers, that fortunately isn't too long. There's a Gasthaus at each side of the top, both with elaborate painted scenes on the exterior walls. The southern one has historical pictures, including the arrival of American tanks near the end of World War II, with the building in flames.

Even though it's pretty low by Alpine standards, the Fern Pass is the closest mountain pass for many Germans, and always has a lot of tour bus traffic. To accommodate all the traffic, the north side has new tunnel work that leads quickly toward Lermoos and back to Germany at Garmisch, or on to Reutte.

Just across the German border at Reutte is Fussen, and Ludwig's castle **Neuschwanstein,** alongside the older castle, **Hohenschwangau.**

If there's time for one Bayrisch baroque church, choose the one at **Rottenbuch,** just a few kilometers north of Oberammergau. It's just off the main road through a low arch gate. Typically, baroque churches are very plain on the outside with no stained glass. But the inside of Rottenbuch is astonishing. Elaborate carving and plaster detail have run riot. It's delightfully flamboyant. The frescoes cast a rosy glow, much cozier than the famous **Wies Kirche** only ten kilometers away. Tours never go to Rottenbuch, probably because buses can't get through the village gate.

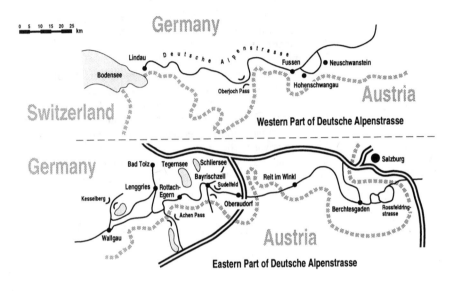

Western Part of Deutsche Alpenstrasse

Eastern Part of Deutsche Alpenstrasse

Deutsche Alpenstrasse

The southern border of Germany, and of Bayern, is where the Alps begin. The big stuff is all south of Germany. In fact, the **Zugspitze,** the highest point in Germany, is on the Austrian border.

In fits and starts, Germany has been constructing a road along the border, called the Deutsche Alpenstrasse. Little of it bears comparison with the high Alps. But a few parts are interesting and are popular with German motorcyclists. The best part by far is a little loop, the Rossfeldringstrasse on the mountain above Salzburg and Berchtesgaden.

As a well-promoted vacation area, the Bayern region is full of hotels and restaurants. One less-trafficked village is **Lenggries,** northeast of the town of Garmisch-Partenkirchen, and just a few kilometers from Austria. From Lenggries, a hardly used one-lane road goes west along the Alp foothills past sturdy Bayrisch farmhouses, the kind with the barn attached to the house. It's signed to Jachenau, and on to Wallgau (see below) and Garmisch.

South of Lenggries is the low Achen Pass leading directly to the Inntal in Austria and across to the Zillertal and Gerlos Pass.

A large, multi-storied, full-service hotel in Lenggries is the **Brauneck;** D-8172 Lenggries, phone 080/ 42 20 21. Nearby, a smaller Gasthof is the **Lenggrieser Hof;** D-8172 Lenggries, phone 080/ 42 87 74.

Trip 44 Deutsche Alpenstrasse West

Distance	*About 110 kilometers from Lindau to Fussen*
Terrain	*Gently sweeping asphalt, one tight climb*
Highlights	*Bucolic countryside, some traffic, photogenic towns, Oberjoch Pass (1180 meters)*

Lindau is a picturesque island town in Bodensee, the very large lake called Lake Constance in English, which is really part of the Rhein River, downstream from all those good passes in Switzerland and just west of Bayern. There's a causeway onto Lindau for trains and vehicles. The trains come in frontward, and exit backward, or vice versa. Other vehicles have to park and turn around to leave. The town is all foot traffic. There is marked motorcycle parking.

East from Lindau, the Deutsche Alpenstrasse makes a pleasant sweeping run along the Austrian border. Green meadows and farms. No big mountains.

At Immenstadt a dead end valley cuts south into the Alps and toward Austria. A part of it, called Klein Walsertal, actually is in Austria, but you can't get to the rest of Austria from it.

Heading east, the road climbs up the only really good twisties, the Oberjoch Pass, only to run into the Austrian border at 1180 meters elevation. Straight ahead, another small pass, Gaichtberg (1093 meters), leads down to Lechtal and Reutte in Austria (see Trip 43).

Meanwhile, the Deutsche Alpenstrasse detours north in Germany to Fussen, site of Ludwig's Neuschwanstein castle, where it sort of ends, to resume farther east beyond Garmisch-Partenkirchen.

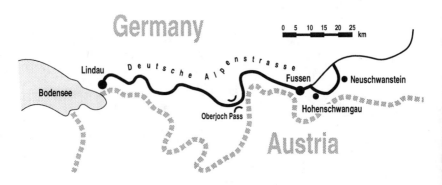

Trip 45 Deutsche Alpenstrasse East

· ·

Distance	*About 200 kilometers*
Terrain	*Some rough narrow, some sweeping*
Highlights	*Cute villages, popular biking roads, Wallgau, Kesselberg, Sudelfeld,* ★ *Rossfeldringstrasse (1536 meters)*

About 12 kilometers east of Garmisch-Partenkirchen on the road toward Innsbruck, a fork goes north to some interesting riding and a delightful picture-perfect Bayrisch village, **Wallgau.** It's close to all the tourists in Garmisch, but hardly touched by them. Several buildings are elaborately painted, including the Post Hotel. The inside of the hotel is as interesting as the outside, and so is the food. Locals have *weiss Wurst,* a sausage made of white meats. Try *Grill Teller,* on the menu at most Bayrisch and Austrian restaurants. *Grill Teller* means a plate of grilled meats, usually five or six kinds, garnished with interesting vegetables.

Before heading on east, a German rider would suggest going north from Wallgau a few kilometers around a lake, Walchensee, famous for windsurfing, to climb a little mountain called **Kesselberg.** The tight sweepers of Kesselberg attract motorcyclists from all of Bayern. So many, in fact, that the road has been closed to southbound motorcycles on weekends and holidays. There's a rest area turnout on the inside of a long sweeper that's a *Tofftreffpunkt.* The village of Kochel, at the north base of Kesselberg, has attractive country hotels.

Back to the Deutsche Alpenstrasse. From the north edge of Wallgau, a tiny, rough, one-lane toll road heads east along the border toward Achen Pass (941 meters). Before it gets to the pass, it becomes a sweeping modern highway.

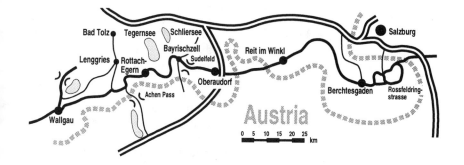

Once again, straight ahead leads into Austria over little Achen Pass, a wonderful way to get to the Inntal below Innsbruck and the Zillertal without any traffic. (Into Austria, the Achen Pass road skirts an Alpine lake with many hotels, then makes a sweeping descent into the Inntal. A hairpin on the descent, called the Kanzel curve, has a restaurant with a magnificent view of the Inntal and the Zillertal).

From the Achen Pass, which actually is already in Austria but before the border station, the Deutsche Alpenstrasse goes north again toward a lake, Tegernsee, which has too much traffic. At Rottach-Egern another bit of one-lane, rough pavement heads south, then north toward another lake with too much traffic, Schliersee. (Schliersee is known in history as the site of the "Night of the Long Knives," when, in the mid-thirties, Hitler turned on the brownshirts after they helped him rise to power, and had them killed.)

East from Schliersee toward Bayrischzell, the Alpenstrasse again becomes a modern road—for a while. And from Bayrischzell, another road heads south into Austria and the Inntal over another little pass, Ursprung (849 meters).

But the best is yet to come: Sudelfeld.

East from Bayrischzell, the road climbs and sweeps in a fashion so delightful that it attracts motorcyclists by the hundreds. On weekends, every corner and the little restaurant at the top is full of motorcyclists watching friends sweep back and forth. So much sweeping, in fact, that the local authorities got the road closed to motorcycles. Court cases got it opened again, but with a speed limit.

Funny thing. The great sweeping road just *ends,* or almost does, at a little, narrow toll tunnel that leads down into the Inntal. It's possible to turn off just before the tunnel and head down another narrow, winding road, past a Gasthaus with a pleasant terrace, down to the Inntal town of Oberaudorf on the German side of the Austrian border. Another end of the Deutsche Alpenstrasse.

From Oberaudorf, the best bet is to head straight on east into Austria, over the Inn River (which is the border). About 25 kilometers into Austria, cross back into Germany at **Reit im Winkl,** a village with many cute buildings decorated in Bavarian style. Here the Deutsche Alpenstrasse takes off again in good sweeping style toward Berchtesgaden. (★ South of Reit im Winkl, a wide, smooth Austrian road winds easily through mountains to Lofer and the roads of Trip 48.) Berchtesgaden is touristy.

On the mountain above Berchtesgaden is the best part of the whole Deutsche Alpenstrasse, the **Rossfeldringstrasse.** This trip of about 25 kilometers is high dancing along the Austrian border, with gorgeous views across Salzburg and its valley to the high Tannengebirge mountains in Austria and in the other direction, over Berchtesgaden. There are several restaurants on the ring road. To get up on the ring from Berchtesgaden, follow the signs to Obersalzberg, a steep climb in the direction of Hitler's **Eagles Nest.** The Rossfeldringstrasse turns off, and then there's a toll booth! In fact, there are two toll booths, one at each end of the toll part of the ring road.

From the ring road there's a well-kept secret way down into Austria with easy access to the Austrian Autobahn. It's pretty and fun and hardly ever used by anyone. Just below the northerly toll booth, a small road heads north. That's it. It has no significant marking, but it goes to a tiny border crossing, and then down to the Austrian mountain town, Durrnberg, site of the famous Salzburg salt mines, then on down to come out in the valley of the Salzach River at the Austrian village of Hallein. It's much easier to get to the Rossfeldringstrasse on this road from Hallein, just south of Salzburg, than from Germany through Berchtesgaden. From Hallein, Austria, look for the new bridge looping over the main street and up the mountainside just north of the old town. The new bridge is the road.

Hordes of tourists visit the salt mines at Durrnberg, but they all come up a little cable car from Hallein, not the road.

Hotel Post in Wallgau is a beautiful place to sample Bayerische food as well as architecture. And the road north over Kesselberg isn't bad either.

Austria East of the Tirol

Central Austria south of Salzburg is the very narrow waist of the country, just over 100 kilometers across, from Berchtesgaden in Germany to Italy. Innsbruck, Tirol, and Vorarlberg are in the west, and Wien (Vienna) is to the east. Since the narrow waist area is all high mountains with many good north-south pass roads, there's a lot of good riding.

There are millions of Germans on one side and millions of Italians on the other side of Austria's narrow waist, all busy going back and forth across little Austria, such a short distance across that they need not stop for even a WC, let alone gas. Except that prudent Austria has concluded that most of this north-south traffic should pay a toll. A couple of the roads are actually private enterprise endeavors.

Austrian private enterprise has also provided a plethora of tourist accommodations. In the first two trips described here, there's a Gasthaus on practically every corner, with Zimmer Frei's in between. Most hotels are attractive Austrian mountain style, with huge roofs, balconies garlanded with flower boxes, and interesting illustrations painted on exterior walls. They almost guarantee good food, attentive service, and spotless,

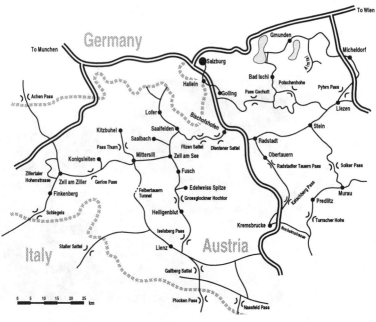

attractive accommodations. Many have elaborate carved wood and wrought iron detailing. There are so many establishments, all so inviting, that any traveler with an economic bent must wonder how they can possibly produce a return on what has to be a very large investment. To an American mind they just don't make economic sense, but they surely are nice.

Most of the hotels spend as much on cooking as on decoration. Area sweet specialties besides *Apfel Strudel* include *Toffel Strudel* (more of a custard base), both with vanilla sauce or the more standard whipped cream. *Kaiser Schmarrn* is a crepe-like concoction smothered in fruit. Practically every menu will have a *Grill Teller*, or mixed grill platter. Sometimes it's good to ask for recommendations. Find out what is just out of the oven, or is specially prepared.

The **Hotel Glocknerhof** is spectacularly set in the high mountain village of Heiligenblut on the south side of the Grossglockner. It hangs on the mountain edge at the entrance to the village with views of the very Austrian village church (tall steeple) and craggy mountains across the green *Molltal* (valley) below. Even the indoor swimming pool has sweeping mountain views. The interior is spacious and charming modern mountain design. A-9844 Heiligenblut; phone 048/ 24 2244.

Four hotels in central Austria advertise themselves as *4 Hauser fur 2 Rader*, or "four houses for two wheels." They specialize in serving motorcyclists. Each is different. They are completely adequate and moderately priced. You can be sure that some part of the family running each is a motorcycle enthusiast, and that all involved will speak motorcycle.

Landhaus Jausern, A-5753 Saalbach, phone 065/ 41 7341. It's high in a dead end valley just north of Zell am See and south of Salzburg. From the main road into Saalbach, turn south. Landhaus Jausern is behind and above a larger hotel.

Hotel Iselsbergerhof, A-9991 Iselsberg, phone 048/ 52 64112. It's on the low pass road of the same name south of the Grossglockner and just north of Lienz.

Hotel Solaria, A-5562 Obertauern, phone 064/ 56 250. This is at the top of a moderately high pass (1740 meters) in ski country, just an hour south of Salzburg. Balconies have views of snowy slopes. It's just off the main pass road. The turn is marked with a motorcycle for a sign. Fun place if it isn't snowing, or even if it is.

Motorradhotel Hubertushof, Mariazellerstrasse 45, A-8623 Aflenz-Kurort, phone 038/ 61 3131. This hotel is at the far east end of the Alps (on Trip 49) closer to Wien, just south of Mariazell and just north of Bruck an der Mur. The owner is a dealer for several brands of bikes. Aflenz-Kurort is an attractive village nestled in Alpine foothills, bypassed by the main highway, with nice public pools and baths. It hardly ever sees an American.

Trip 46 Achen Pass From Germany

Distance	*About 170 kilometers from Germany via Zillertaler Hohenstrasse, Schlegeis, Gerlos Pass, to Grossglockner*
Terrain	*Good sweepers, narrow erratic road on Zillertaler Hohenstrasse, old Gerlos*
Highlights	*Lovely farms and villages, fun roads with some traffic spots, good hotels and cafes. Includes: Achen Pass (941 meters), Zillertaler Hohenstrasse, Schlegeis (1784 meters), Gerlos Pass (1507 meters), Konigsleiten, Pass Thurn (1273 meters)*

The Achen Pass (see Trip 45, Deutsche Alpenstrasse) sweeps magnificently down into the Inntal, and it's possible to proceed from it right up the Zillertal, a valley with every imaginable shade of green. The Zillertal is decorated with a narrow gauge railroad, sometimes sporting a chuffing steam-powered train. At Zell am Ziller, the Gerlos Pass road leaves the Zillertal and starts climbing a finger valley to the east.

But before that, at Ried, the Zillertaler Hohenstrasse climbs the mountainside to the west, where it hangs and dances in a one-lane game in and out of the tree line, offering dazzling views of the yellow-green, blue-green, and green-green quilt below and the Gerlos Pass road snaking up opposite. It finally comes back down in the Zillertal at Ramsberg. There's a toll.

Head farther south on up the Zillertal past Mayrhofen and Finkenberg. Just above Finkenberg, all traffic is directed to a

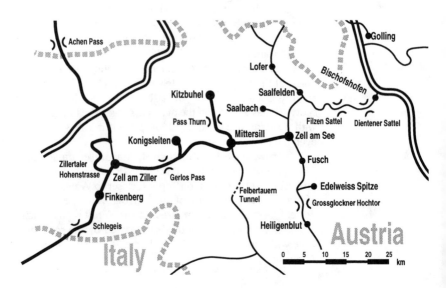

High on the Zillertaler Hohenstrasse, last night's snow has touched the fir trees and mountain tops. Across the Zillertal, the Gerlos Pass road can be seen climbing east up its finger canyon.

new road and tunnel going farther up the valley. The old road, to the right, is the correct choice. It snakes through a gorge with overhanging cliffs. Snuggled against the cliffs is the **Gasthaus Jodburg;** A-6292 Finkenberg 595; phone 0528/ 518110.

Farther up, a toll road with a one-way-at-a-time traffic light leads into the high Schlegeis. Near the end of the road, a gravel drive leads up above a lake to the **Dominikushutte,** a restaurant with a view of Italian mountain peaks. It's a good turn-around spot.

Back down at Zell am Ziller, the Gerlos climbs east through a tourist town of the same name, Gerlos. Near the top there's a toll gate onto a new swooping alignment that supposedly offers views of the Krimmler waterfall. The views are from quite a distance. Turn north and take the old road instead. It bounces and weaves and heaves in great sport down the mountain. Part is narrow. Some bridges are wooden. There may be signs advising (in German, of course) that on some days and at some hours, work may be in progress. Bikes can probably get through even if work is in progress. Certainly Gasthaus operators on the old road will hope so!

Near the top of the Gerlos, just about where the toll road splits off, is an opportunity to climb a bit higher to a ski village called **Konigsleiten,** with a couple of good hotels. **Hotel Gasthof Ursprung;** A-5742 Konigsleiten, Wald-Pinzgau; phone 06564/ 82538271, FAX 06564/ 82538.

From the Gerlos, it's straight ahead east to Zell am See and the Grossglockner, skirting the high Tauern mountain spine of Austria to the south, and the Kitzbuhel Alps to the north. At Mittersill, little Pass Thurn joins from the north, and the big Felbertauern toll tunnel road joins from the south, coming out from under the Hohe Tauern mountains. The Felbertauern tunnel is the main north-south, all-weather connection across the waist of Austria, parallel to the Grossglockner.

Four hotels in Austria advertise themselves as "4 Hauser fur 2 Rader," four houses for two wheels. Hotel Solaria, high atop the Obertauern Pass, and set back from the main road, is easy for a biker to find.

The narrow old road above Mayrhofen up to Schlegeis, hugs the cliffs under overhanging rocks.

Trip 47 Passes From Italy

Distance   From Italy to Grossglockner, via Staller Sattel, about 65 kilometers; via Plocken Pass, about 50 kilometers; via Nassfeld Pass, about 60 kilometers

Terrain   Via Staller Sattel, good sweepers; via Plocken Pass, pleasant road; via Nassfeld Pass, pleasant road

Highlights   Via ★ Staller Sattel (2048 meters), pretty country, hotels; via Plocken Pass, quick connection; via Nassfeld Pass (1530 meters), good escape from Italian autostrada

★ Staller Sattel is the fun one-way-at-a-time pass into Austria from the Dolomites in Italy (see Dolomites, Trip 38). It comes down into Austria from the one-way part, past the **Tandlerstub'n** hotel restaurant in St. Jakob, joining the Felbertauern road south of the tunnel, and goes on into the major city of the Ost (east) Tirol, Lienz. (The Ost Tirol is the part

that voted to rejoin Austria in the 1920s after it had been awarded to Italy at Versailles. It is separated from the rest of the Austrian Tirol by the Sud Tirol, still part of Italy.)

From Lienz, a fine sweeper climbs the Iselsberg Pass (site of one of the motorcycle hotels) toward Heiligenblut and the Grossglockner. The Iselsberg provides the last (or first) glimpses of the Dolomites.

East of the Dolomites, east of Cortina d'Ampezzo, two seldom-used passes—Plocken and Nassfeld—cross from Italy into Austria (they aren't usually called by their Italian names, Passo di Monte Croce Carnico and Passo di Pramollo).

The Plocken especially has an exciting climb up out of Italy in layered switchbacks through forests. The Nassfeld is just ten kilometers off the autostrada/Autobahn between Venezia and Wien. It's a wonderful way to escape the diesel trucks and buses of the autostrada. Both passes enter a seldom-traversed Austrian valley of pleasant interest. From it, the Gailberg Sattel connects directly to Lienz in the East Tirol, Iselsberg, and the Grossglockner.

The Plocken Pass makes an audacious climb out of Italy into Austria, leading toward the Grossglockner.

Trip 48   Grossglockner

Distance   About 200 kilometers over Grossglockner and Radstadter Tauern; about 170 kilometers over Katschberg, Nockalmstrasse, Turracher Hohe and Solker Pass

Terrain   Every kind of mountain road: tight, sweeping, narrow hairpins over six major passes and a couple of lesser ones

Highlights   Exhilarating riding and scenery. Includes: Grossglockner Hochtor (2505 meters), Edelweiss Spitze (2577 meters), Filzen Sattel (1291 meters), Dientener Sattel (1357 meters), Radstadter Tauern Pass (1739 meters), Katschberg Pass (1641 meters), Nockalmstrasse, Eisentalhohe (2042 meters), Turracher Hohe (1763 meters), Solker Pass (1790 meters), Rottenmanner Tauern Pass (1265 meters)

★ ★

The Grossglockner Hochalpenstrasse, Grossglockner for short, is one of the major play roads of the Alps. In crossing the highest spine of the Austrian Alps, it combines every test of driving skill: hairpins, sweepers, jig-jags, cobblestones, steep descents, narrow ledges, sometimes ice and snow and hanging clouds of fog,

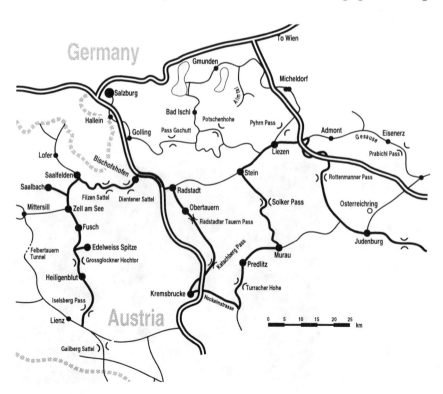

along with spectacular views and plenty of restaurants. It's only a half-day's drive from Munchen and the big cities of northern Italy, and even less from Salzburg, so it is a testing spot for the latest machines and visiting drivers. And it's private enterprise.

Yes, it's a private toll road. And fairly expensive. Typically, the Austrians in cute costumes at the toll booths will take any kind of money. Once through the toll booths, it's possible to play back and forth and up and down to the heart's content, even stay at one of the several hotels. If a return trip is anticipated from outside the toll booths, it's possible to arrange a slightly reduced price in advance. Environmentalists are raising some Cain about limiting access to the Grossglockner Hochalpenstrasse—too many tourists tramping about looking for Edelweiss—but private enterprise and the profit motive have kept it open so far. (Sorry, Austrians don't know the popular song, "Edelweiss," from *The Sound of Music.*) This is the Austrian state of Karnten, which we English speakers call Carinthia.

The approach from the north is up the Fuschertal, a lush green valley, from Zell am See and Bruck, past the village of Fusch. Then the climb.

There are two short tunnels and two humps across the top. The north hump is called Fuscher Tor (Fusch Gate) and the other Hoch (high) Tor, with a high Alpine valley between the two, where the road often cuts through deep snow banks.

Near the Fuscher Tor, what looks like a restaurant parking lot leads to the snaking little road up to the highest point, Edelweiss Spitze. The road's worth the trip. The view from the restaurant at the top is reward enough. Above, all around are high peaks, and below, bits of ribbon roads. To the south, the ribbon, not really a ribbon but a string, works across the Alpine meadows. Until August it's just a slit in deep snow banks. Then it disappears in a tunnel. To the north, the road seems to weave to the mountain's edge and then disappear into the Fuschertal.

Time for hot chocolate.

The high stuff. From Edelweiss Spitze on the Grossglockner, the pass road is a ribbon across the high Alpine valleys, disappearing into tunnels to the south (left) and dropping off the edge to the north.

About halfway down the south side, well below the Hochtor, a road leads about nine kilometers around the mountain to a huge parking garage called Franz Josefs Hohe. There's a view of the Grossglockner itself, the big mountain that's supposed to look like a big bell, and a cable car ride down onto the ice of the Pasterze Glacier. Bikes can usually find a nook or cranny or a piece of sidewalk to park on outside the huge garage. Some of the road to the garage and back is in concrete snow sheds.

Just outside the southern toll booths is the high village of **Heiligenblut** (Holy Blood), whose name sounds better untranslated. Besides the Glocknerhof, there are several other hotels and Gasthaus possibilities. There's often an evening brass band concert in the little town square, backed by a fountain made of huge mountain crystals. The little church at Heiligenblut is a good example of the original Austrian Gothic that has not been baroqued. The memorials in it illustrate the horrible costs of 20th century wars to families of the village.

South from Heiligenblut, down the Molltal, is the Iselsberg Pass up and over toward Lienz and Italy. North of the Grossglockner, and north of Zell am See about five kilometers, is the turnoff to Saalbach and one of the motorcycle hotels. A few kilometers farther north is Saalfelden and the pleasant Austrian roads to Reit im Winkl on the Deutsche Alpenstrasse.

But the Austrian trip heads east from Saalfelden toward the Filzen Sattel and Dientener Sattel. The Sattel roads bypass Maria Alm, a beautiful village. Beyond it, the Sattel roads climb steeply and irregularly. Parts have been improved recently, but the old sections are the most fun. All this is just south of Berchtesgaden and the Rossfeldringstrasse in Germany. The countryside is rural, remote, and tourist-free all the way across the Sattels and down a twisting gorge to Bischofshofen. The road bypasses Bischofshofen, connecting straight across the Salzach River to the Tauern Autobahn high on the mountain opposite.

The Tauern Autobahn crosses the Alpine spine in a toll tunnel. But it's free up to the tunnel, so you might as well take it south about 20 kilometers to the exit for Radstadt and Radstadter Tauern Pass. The road up the pass bypasses the town, Radstadt, then starts up a pleasant valley on new alignment that's almost too nice, to Untertauern where it darts into a gorge and climbs steeply and sharply alongside a raging frothing torrent, to emerge at Obertauern, site of one of the motorcycle hotels—the one with the motorcycle beside the road for a sign. A stop at the hotel for a stay or refreshment is an invitation to view the high Alpine countryside from off the main road, which is kind of commercialized.

On the south side, the Radstadter Tauern Pass only comes down to castled **Mauterndorf** at 1122 meters, where a jog south zips right back up the Katschberg Pass, high atop the Autobahn tunnel. The Katschberg comes down beside the

Autobahn as it emerges from the tunnel onto fantastic concrete viaducts, practically roofing the narrow valley.

Here comes an interesting and rarely traveled pass road, the Nockalmstrasse, another private enterprise toll adventure. To catch it, it's necessary to duck under the huge Autobahn structure at Kremsbrucke and head up the side valley to Innerkrems where the Nockalmstrasse heads south. It climbs and twists up and down and over through wild, otherwise inaccessible Alpine highlands, for 34 kilometers. As at the Grossglockner, once inside the toll gates, it's permissible to play back and forth between the toll gates, and eat and/or stay at the facilities along the road. The south end of the Nockalmstrasse is also the south end of the next pass, Turracher Hohe. A more than 90-degree turn back up the mountain brings the very steep (23%) climb up the Turracher Hohe, to the ski hotels at its top.

The north side of the Turracher Hohe is sweeping and less steep, down to a little village, Predlitz in the Murtal. A jog east to Murau, and then north, leads to the Solker Pass. It's another obscure, seldom-traveled, often no more than one lane, road. Just over the top on the north side, up a gravel driveway, is a good restaurant, the **Erherzog Johann Hutte.**

From Stein, at the north end of the Solker Pass, it's about 40 kilometers east down the Ennstal to the base of the Rottenmanner Tauern Pass. There's a pretty good sized town named Rottenmanner, but the pass is farther east, and starts south over the Tauern mountains at Trieben. The north side of the pass has good sweepers. The south is a more old-fashioned alignment through farmland. From the south end at Pols, a back road leads east in a few kilometers to the **Osterreichring,** site of the Austrian Gran Prix.

South of the Osterreichring, southeast from the town of Judenburg at Weisskirchen, the Gaberl Sattel road goes up and over to Graz. A good quality, traffic-free road sweeps along the south base of the Tauern mountains west from the Rottenmanner Tauern Pass at Oberzeiring.

It's only six more hairpins like this from Fuscher Tor on the Grossglockner to Edelweiss Spitze.

Trip 49 Near Vienna (Wien)

Distance	*About 300 kilometers from Salzburg to Aflenz-Kurort*
Terrain	*Gently sweeping over low passes*
Highlights	*Popular, scenic lakes and lower mountains, occasional narrow roads, popular motorcycle cafe at Kalte Kuchl. Includes: Pass Gschutt (969 meters), Potschenhohe (992 meters), Aflenzer Seeberg (1253 meters), Lahn Sattel (1015 meters), Kalte Kuchl, Gaberl Sattel (1547 meters).*

East of Salzburg and east of the Solker Pass, almost as far as Wien, are lovely lakes and low mountains that have captured the hearts of romanticists. Names like Salzkammergut, St. Wolfgang See, Bad Ischl (a favorite of Kaiser Franz Joseph up to World War I), Gesause, Mariazell and Raxalpe are famous. Some roads are nice. Some, not so nice. Nothing is exotic. Nothing is like the Dolomites or Andermatt or the Grossglockner. Some of the valleys are rather tedious and industrial.

South of Salzburg on the Autobahn, past Hallein where the road climbs up to the Rossfeldringstrasse, at the Golling Ausfahrt, a wonderfully pleasant sweeping road heads up and east through a fine mountain village, **Abtenau,** and on across low Pass Gschutt, to a popular mountain lake, Halstatter See. Almost the whole thing is new, sweeping, smooth asphalt. North around the Halstatter See leads to another lowly pass, Potschenhohe and to Bad Aussee. South around Halstatter See

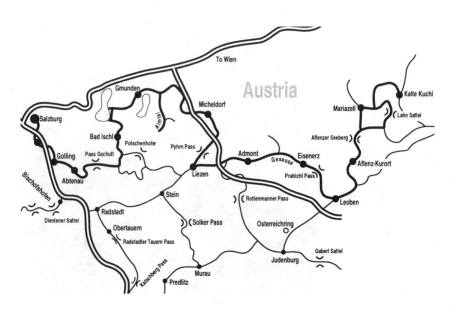

is a smaller road that takes a tunnel around a village, then makes a steep rough climb to Bad Aussee.

Bad Ischl and St. Wolfgang See are north of this route on the main road east from Salzburg. North of Bad Ischl are some nice roads climbing small passes between lovely lakes. There's one between Bad Ischl and Attersee, and one between Attersee and Gmunden, and one between Gmunden and Micheldorf. Midway on the latter is Scharnstein. South from Scharnstein, an interesting dead end road up the Almtal leads to a tight, twisting climb through the woods on a one-lane paved road to a high restaurant-hotel called the **Hochberghaus**; A-4645 Grunau im Almtal-Salzkammergut; phone 076/ 168477. The road up is called the Bergstrasse Farrenau.

The main road south from Micheldorf climbs over the low Pyhrn Pass (954 meters) to the Gesause, a road listed in all the guide books as scenic. It's an uneventful road wandering farther east toward the Prabichl Pass at Eisenerz. The countryside around Eisenerz and the Prabichl looks like it's been strip mined, and Eisenerz looks like a "company town" in Wales or West Virginia. Steyr, home of Puch, is downstream from Eisenerz and the Prabichl, the source of its iron ore.

The Alps have their last fling about 90 kilometers short of Wien. The area is easily reached from the Motorradhotel Hubertushof at Aflenz-Kurort, listed above. The *Tofftreffpunkt,* for riders of Wien and eastern Austria, who know where the nearby good roads are, is an intersection with a Gasthof called **Kalte Kuchl.** Despite its name ("cold kitchen"), it has good hot food, and the terraces are full of bikers on weekends. The two passes of note, Lahn Sattel and Aflenzer Seeberg, are between Aflenz-Kurort and Kalte Kuchl.

(*Kurort* means "cure village" and the "cure" usually refers to the local water. Drink it or bathe in it, or have mud packs of it, or . . .)

Almost at the gates of Wein (Vienna), the most easterly passes of the Alps attract motorcyclists from the city. The Gasthous at Kalte Kuckl is right where a couple of good roads intersect.

On the roads around Andermatt, it's possible to ride one exotic pass after another, without ever getting mixed up with cities or dense traffic. Here, the north side of the Grimsel Pass snakes down to Gletsch, no more than a couple of stone buildings, where the Furka Pass road starts climbing back up and east to Andermatt. (See Trips 1 through 4.)

Special Little Roads

In the Alps are many special little roads that might have been put there just for motorcyclists to play on. It has taken me many enjoyable years to discover them; this book is my tribute to the joy they have given me. For your convenience, they are arranged according to the regions they occupy. But some of these roads are so exceptional, their potential for enjoyment so great, that they deserve to be singled out and given special consideration by any motorcyclist.

All the roads I'll mention here are described elsewhere in the book, in their appropriate geographical context. Most of them don't go anywhere in particular, certainly nowhere of commercial importance. They are not necessarily high or awesome, although some are both. Most of them have stretches that are only one lane wide. They are all paved. Some of them are short and some long. Some remain obscure even though they're close to major tourist areas or routes.

Special Little Roads in Switzerland

1. Pragel Pass between the towns of Glarus and Schwyz. (Part of Andermatt Trip 4.)

2. Glaubenbuelen Pass between the towns of Schupfheim and Giswil. (Part of The Berner Oberland Trip 6.)

3. Glaubenberg Pass between the towns of Entlebuch and Sarnen. (Also part of The Berner Oberland Trip 6.)

Special Little Roads in France

1. Cormet de Roselend and Col du Pre between the towns of Bourg St. Maurice and Beaufort. (Part of Trip 13, Mont Blanc region.)

2. Col de Joux Plane between the towns of Morzine and Samoens. (Part of Trip 15, Lac d'Annecy region.)

Special Little Roads in Italy

1. Colle San Carlo between the towns of Morgex and La Thuile. (Part of Trip 13, Mont Blanc region.)

2. Passo di Croce Domini between the towns of Bagolino and Breno. (Part of Trip 31, Riva and Lago di Garda.)

3. Passo di Vivione between the towns of Forno Allione and Shilpario. (Part of Trip 31, Riva and Lago di Garda.)

4. Wurz Joch (Passo di Erbe) between the towns of St. Martin and Bressanone (Brixen). (Part of Trip 36, The Dolomites.)

5. Passo Manghen between the towns of Cavalese and Borgo. (Part of Trip 36, The Dolomites.)

Special Little Roads in Austria

1. Furka Joch between the towns of Rankweil and Damuls. (Part of Trip 41, Liechtenstein, Santis, and the Arlberg.)

2. Hahntenn Joch between the towns of Imst and Elmen. (Part of Trip 43, Austrian Tirol.)

3. Haiming Joch between the village of Haiming and Ochsengarten. (Part of Trip 43, Austrian Tirol.)

4. Zillertaler Hohenstrasse between the towns of Ried and Ramsberg. (Part of Trip 46, Austria East of the Tirol.)

If You Have Only a Little Time

It's better to ride a little in the Alps than not at all. So if you just have a few days, which country, which roads, should you aim for? Where will you have the most fun and see the most in just a few days? A week?

First Andermatt, Switzerland. It's covered right at the beginning of this book. The mountains are spectacular, the roads exciting, facilities plentiful, and there's no big city traffic to worry about. You can get to the area quickly by Autobahn, and then leave the Autobahn and traffic behind. There are several full days of riding around Andermatt.

Second, the Dolomites in northern Italy. They're covered in the section of the same name. Like those around Andermatt, the mountains are special and the roads are right up in them. Facilities are plentiful, and there is no big city traffic. You can get there quickly from the Brennero Autostrada. Several more full days of riding.

Just remember the warning in the front of this book. Alpinitis is contagious.

Other European Goals

Are all the great roads in the Alps? Aren't there any others?

Of course. But truly, all suffer in comparison to the Alps. Try the roads anywhere else, as many have. They may seem pretty good. Sometimes the scenery is almost as good. Then come back to the Alps. There's no getting around it. The roads of the Alps are the best. Nothing compares. Except Corsica.

Other areas tested, in no particular order:

Norway

A real challenge. There is a lot of it, about 2400 kilometers from Oslo to the North Cape. And there's almost nobody there. Cruise posters illustrate how lovely the fjords are. They don't show how tedious and occasional the roads are. There is lots of water. But facilities are few, modest, and very expensive. One-lane roads with trucks and buses going both ways cling to the edges of the fjords. A overlay of skid marks is a constant reminder of what may be around endless blind corners. From the fjords, the roads climb up into a tundra-like crossing to the next fjord. And Norway is a long haul from the core of Europe. It's possible to cut some of the travel time to and from Norway by using ferries from Newcastle in the north of England or from the Netherlands, to Bergen; or from Kiel, in north Germany to Oslo. All of the ferry connections take about 18 hours. For about the price of a night in a modest hotel (less than any hotel

On Corsica, roads like the Scala de Santa Regina lead from mountain tops to quiet sandy beaches.

in Norway), it's possible to get a tiny cabin on the ferry and eliminate a bunch of flat road time to boot. It is heady to ride all night in daylight. There can be a bit of a high about 1 a.m.

Pyrenees

Every once in a while, the high mountains that separate Spain and France look almost Alpine. A few of the passes are Alpine in height, and some of the snow bowls could double for those in the Alps. What's missing is the culture and the road network. The tiny independent country of Andorra has adequate facilities, and some, up above its main valley road, are very pleasant. As a tax-free country, it is jammed with tourists loading their cars with everything imaginable (including new motorcycles), and with trucks hauling the stuff in so the tourists can buy it and haul it out. Americans are unknown in Andorra. The Spanish side is no longer cheap.

★ ★ Corsica

Corsica, the Mediterranean island, is as good as the Alps. Endless roads twist over high mountain passes, past snow capped peaks, down to jagged, cliff-hanging roads with white sand beaches, good hotels, and both Italian and French food. Since the 18th century, this Mediterranean island has been French, and in French it's called La Corse. Even though it's only about 200 kilometers long and 100 wide, it has enough roads to keep the most ardent enthusiast busy for more than a week. It's possible to stay in mountain forests surrounded by snowy peaks, or on the beach with mountain roads at the door. It's a major destination of European motorcyclists. But no Americans of any sort. It's still possible to be the first American some of the residents have ever seen. Reach Corsica by ferry from Livorno, Italy (the port for Pisa and Firenze), or from Nice, France. From either, it's about five hours.

Sardinia (Sardegna)

Visible from the south of Corsica, Sardinia is not nearly as rugged, and doesn't make the cut.

I.F.M.A.

The International Bicycle and Motorcycle Show (International Fahrrad und Motorrad Ausstellung), held every even-numbered year in Koln (Cologne), Germany, is the biggest event of its kind. It's held late in September. Anything remotely related to motorcycles or motorcycling will be there for show and for sale.

★ Isle of Man

Since the first years of the 20th century, the first week of June has been motorcycle week on the Isle of Man. The adjective for

Through the Gorges de la Restonica is one of the high mountain roads on the little Mediterranean island of Corsica. Corsica has more roads than a good rider can cover in a week, including passes through snowy mountains like this.

it is Manx, for cats and for Nortons. The island is in the Irish Sea, west of England, north of Wales, and east of Ireland. The collection of enthusiasts from all over the world is a joy to be part of. The major TT races are the first weekend of June, with practice during the prior week. Practice can be as much fun as the racing. The course is all public roads about the island, totaling about 30 miles. It's open to the public except during practice hours and during races. The course is open to all on the first Sunday in June. It's come to be known as Mad Sunday, as too many amateurs overestimate their skills. The atmosphere is motorcycle-friendly.

Accommodations are working-class British, as is the food. The island has some nice roads to explore besides the course. Access is by ferry from Heysham on the Lancashire coast of England, north of Liverpool, with a weekly run from Dublin. Both take about five hours. Reservations for the ferry are essential, and can be obtained from the Isle of Man Tourist Board in Douglas, phone 0624/ 29914. They do indeed speak English there, but they drive on the left, even on the TT course.

Nurburgring

The historic and famous Nurburgring is often available to riders. It's much longer than most tracks, the north ring being about 14 kilometers, and it sweeps and wiggles through the low Eifel Mountains up near the border of Belgium, about 40 kilometers west of Koblenz. (It's easy for the English speaker to confuse the Nurburgring up north with the Bayrisch city, Nurnberg, where the war crimes trials were held after World War II.)

Many Americans have participated in the driving school held over a period of several days each summer on the Nurburgring by the BMW Clubs of Europe. Contact Werner Briel in Mulheim am der Ruhr, phone 0203/ 358020; Fax 0203/ 376372. The school concentrates on learning the multitudinous curves of the Ring. A reasonable beginning competence is presumed. It's a good place to make European contacts.

So, How About a Bike?

There are several ways to have a bike in the Alps. Each depends on two factors that the user decides: time and money. Usually, a little of one will save a bit of the other.

- borrow or rent
- buy
- ship it from home
- keep a bike there

Borrow or Rent One

It surely would be nice to have a friend in Europe to borrow a bike from. Lacking that, you can rent one.

Bikes are available for rent from many sources. Most of the tour operators who are known in the United States rent bikes to riders who attend their tours. However, several tour operators will also rent motorcycles to riders who are not on tour with them.

BMW rents at the factory in Munchen. (Of course, the bike factories are in Berlin, but THE factory is still by the Olympic Center in Munchen.) They have daily prices with unlimited kilometers, and longer rates with a kilometer charge. The reservations phone in Germany is 089/ 3875 extension 231 or 232.

Bosenberg Motorcycle Excursions in Bad Kreuznach, Germany, rents bikes. Phone Germany 0671/ 67580; FAX 0671/ 67153.

Members of Harley Owners Group can make arrangements to rent a Harley in Europe through H.O.G. in Milwaukee.

Buy One There

Some factors beyond the control of individuals, and even dealers and manufacturers, bear on the choice, and they vary from year to year and season to season.

The rate of exchange is crucial, along with the rules and cost of shipping. In some years American currencies are high and that makes everything in Europe, including motorcycles, seem like a bargain. In such circumstances, shipping a bike from American won't make much sense since they're cheaper in Europe than America and almost all bikes are available for sale.

Then the opposite happens. American currency sinks in relative value and everything is cheaper in America. It then may make sense to ship your bike from America.

There has been one mitigating factor in this game: until now, BMW had not changed its price for factory-delivered machines as fast as the currency had changed. So when dollars were weak, BMW held the price in dollars, with the result that the price for a European-delivered U.S.-specification bike was actually much less than the Europeans were paying for the same machine at the same place and time. And vice versa. When American currency went up in value, it was cheaper to buy on the open market in Europe. There is talk that BMW may terminate its European delivery program in 1993.

Then there's the matter of U.S. specifications. Only the manufacturer can certify to them, and it's practically impossible to get a non-U.S.-spec bike into the U.S. Of course, if the goal is to leave the bike in Europe, then U.S. specs are not so important, unless U.S. registration is desired.

To buy a BMW, the best arrangement has been with a local BMW dealer at home. The price for factory delivery should be the same from any source, unless the dollar should soar in relative value. Then it might be worthwhile to phone Paddy Maddock near Dublin, Ireland. He can sell U.S.-spec BMWs in German marks. Phone Ireland, 01/ 868418. That language he speaks is English.

Dealers all over Europe are selling new and used bikes. Magazines and papers are full of ads, just like in America. Investing some time and patience can result in a good deal. Europeans do have strict vehicle inspection, called TUV in German, that limits modifications and maintains safety and pollution controls. They also have a significant value-added tax. A dealer selling to a non-resident alien should be able to take care of everything including insurance, and possibly, the refund of the value-added tax upon proof of export.

Ship a Bike From Home

Shipping from America can be a good deal, but it's an ever-changing game. What worked well one time may not the next. Shipping by sea, short of taking a bike as baggage, takes time and planning. Usually the bike must be crated, and then it must be forklift handled to the dock, and the process reversed at the other end. Docks are often inconveniently located. Rats can eat the plastic! Freighters may not be on an exact schedule, so time at both ends is required.

So air freight is almost always the choice. With most airlines, bikes must be crated to be flown, but not with Lufthansa. They have had lots of experience shipping motorcycles and know how to transport them safely without crating. They require that you travel on the same flight as your bike. It is fun to get off the airplane in Europe, go around to the freight terminal, go through customs, and ride away from the airport. Agents for other carriers are hungry for business, and are willing to talk both price and crating. Sometimes containers can hold several bikes for the price of one. Prices are related to cubic space needed.

The airline and agent that worked wonders one time may not the next. Call a variety of airline freight agents. One of them may be a biker.

To get your bike out of customs in Europe, it will be necessary to prove you have European insurance, and the customs agent will want to be assured that the bike is just passing through, not being imported. If the bike is legal in America, then it's legal for an American to operate it on holiday in Europe.

If the bike is ever sold to a European, then it will have to be imported with all the taxes and inspections Europeans require.

Keep a Bike in Europe

Sometimes it's harder to find a good air freight deal back from Europe to America. Many Americans are so hooked that they keep bikes in Europe from one holiday to the next. Some rent garages. Some leave them in bonded warehouses. Some leave bikes with cooperative dealers. Then the only problem is how to keep the thing registered in America, while avoiding permanently importing it to Europe.

Motorcycling with a group will introduce you to other like-minded adventurers. Many friendships made through motorcycling last a lifetime. And what better way to savor the adventure than to share it with friends. Here, a group checks its route through Passo Tremalzo, above Pieve. (See Trip 30.)

An Organized Tour?

Most every road is better shared. It's possible to meet new lifelong motorcycle friends on an organized tour. Other smart, creative, attractive, motorcycle crazies like you. If time is limited, the tour folk will take care of the details and leave the riding to you. They just may have some good ideas about where to go and how to get there. And they've had practice helping if something should not go as planned.

Here are several tour operators who specialize in trips through the Alps. They'll even carry the hair dryer.

Beach's Motorcycle Adventures, Ltd.
2763 West River Parkway
Grand Island, NY 14072-2053
Phone: 716-773-4960
Fax: 716-773-5227

Bosenberg Motorcycle Excursions
Mainzer Strasse 54
D-6550 Bad Kreuznach
GERMANY
Phone: (49) 6 716-7312
Fax: (49) 6 716-7153

Desmond Adventures, Inc.
1900 Folsom Street #107
Boulder, CO 80302
Phone: 303-444-5151
Fax: 303-786-8888

Edelweiss Bike Travel
Steinreichweg 1
A-6414 Mieming
AUSTRIA
Phone: (43) 5 264-5690
Fax: (43) 5 264-58533

European Adventures
2 The Circle, Bryn Newydd
Prestatyn, Clwyd LL19 9EU
WALES
Phone: (44) 745-853455
Fax: (44) 745-888919

Jed Halpern's S.A.P Tour
Pilatusstrasse 1; CH Dierikon - 6036
Lucerne
SWITZERLAND
Phone: (41) 4 324-3482
Fax: (41) 4 324-3212

mhs Motorradtouren GmbH
Donnersbergerstrasse 32
D-8000 Munich 19
GERMANY
Phone: (49) 89-168-4888
Fax: (49) 89-166-5549

Motorrad Reisen GmbH
Postfach 44 01 48
D-8000 Munich 44
GERMANY
Phone: (49) 8 939-5768
Fax: (49) 8 934-4832

Team Aventura
Karlsebene 2
D-8924 Steingaden
GERMANY
Phone: (49) 8 862-6161
Fax: (49) 8 862-6161

Von Thielmann Tours
P.O. Box 87764
San Diego, CA 92138
Phone: 619-463-7788 or 619-234-1558
Fax: 619-463-7788

World Motorcycle Tours
14 Forest Avenue
Caldwell, NJ 07006
Phone: 201-226-9107
Fax: 201-226-8106

About the Weather

• •

To give you a sense of what kind of weather to expect on your travels we've listed some cities in the Alpine region with their average high and low seasonal temperatures, and relative humidity.

Table entries are:

Average high temperature/Average low temperature, Relative humidity

(Temperature is given in degrees Fahrenheit)

(Relative humidity is in percent)

	Jan-Mar	April-June	July-Sept	Oct-Dec
Innsbruck, Austria	40/24, 58%	68/46, 43%	75/54, 52%	46/0, 65%
Bordeaux, France	51/36, 73%	69/48, 60%	78/56, 60%	55/40, 80%
Lugano, Switzerland	48/31, 52%	69/50, 53%	80/60, 51%	51/38, 59%

About Money

• •

As of July, 1993, the U.S. dollar related to European currencies as shown in the chart below. Note that currency exchange rates fluctuate daily. This chart is intended only to give you a general idea of relative currency values. Current rates can be found in the business section of many daily newspapers.

One U.S. dollar = AS 12.14 (Austrian schillings)
One U.S. dollar = £ .67 (British pounds)
One U.S. dollar = DM 1.72 (German Deutsche Marks)
One U.S. dollar = F 5.89 (French francs)
One U.S. dollar = L 1597 (Italian lira)
One U.S. dollar = F 1.52 (Swiss francs)

One Austrian schilling = .08 U.S. dollars
One British pound = 1.49 U.S. dollars
One German Deutsche Mark = .58 U.S. dollars
One French franc = .17 U.S. dollars
One Italian lira = .0006 U.S. dollars
One Swiss franc = .66 U.S. dollars

Glossary

aiguille - French word for needle, applied especially to peaks in the Mt. Blanc massif, as Aiguille du Midi

albergo - Italian word for inn or small hotel

Allemagne - the French word for Germany

Alpenglow - the almost flourescent pink glow of snow covered peaks at sunrise and sunset.

Alpenstrasse - German, a road in the Alps, plural is Alpenstrassen

Alpinist - a mountain climber in the Alps; alpinist is a mountain climber in general

Alpinitis - a Hermannism, infected by the Alps

alt, alte - German word for old

aperto - Italian word for open

Apfel - German word for apple

aubergine - French word for eggplant

Ausfahrt - German word for freeway exit (a pedestrian exit is Ausgang)

Ausstellung - German word for exhibition

Autobahn - German word for freeway; plural is Autobahnen

autoroute - French word for freeway

autostrada - Italian word for freeway, plural is autostrade

aux - French preposition, "to the;" hotel Aux Mille Etoiles, Les Marecottes (CH)

bain - French word for bath

basilica - a special name for a large church; not a cathedral

Bayern - German word for Bavaria

Bayrisch - adj. German word for Bavarian

bei - German word, prep. for at or near; Trimbach bei Olten

Berghaus - German for house on a mountain; Berghaus Gurnigel (CH)

Bergstrasse - German for mountain road; Bergstrasse Ferrenau (A)

Berner - German word for Bernese, adj. of Bern (CH)

Bernese - adj. & n. pertaining to Bern

besonder - German word for special

bis - German word, prep., until

bleu - French word for blue

bolognese - Italian adjective for the town Bologna, often applied to a meat sauce on pasta

bourg - French word for village

Brot - German word for bread

Brucke - German word for bridge

Bundesstrasse - German for federal road, *i.e.,* not a freeway

cambio - Italian word for change, exchange

campanile - bell tower

cannelloni - a kind of pasta

cappuccino - Italian coffee with steamed milk

carne - Italian word for meat, flesh

centro - Italian word for center, downtown

certosa - Italian word for charterhouse; Hotel Certosa (I) near Merano, called Karthaus in German

chiuso - Italian word for closed, shut, locked

cognoscente - a connoisseur, one in the know

col - French word for pass, as a mountain pass

corso - Italian word for course, large street; "in corso" is Italian for in progress

creme de la creme - the very choicest

Cyrillic - Slavic alphabet, Russian

Danemark - German word for Denmark; Coupe Danemark, hot fudge sundae

del - Italian "of the" masculine before a consonant

della - Italian "of the" feminine before consonant, singular

demi - French word for half

der - German word for article "the," masculine

des - French prep., "of the"

Deutsch - German word for German; adj., requires declension; Deutsche Alpenstrasse

Deutschland - (D) German word for Germany

deviazione - Italian word for detour

di - Italian word, prep. "of," "by," "with"

d' - French prep., "of," before a vowel

Dolomiten - German word for Dolomites

Dolomiti - Italian word for Dolomites

Dorf - German word for village

drei - German word for three

Edelweiss - German name for Alpine flower

einfach - German word for simple

Eisenbahn - German word for railroad; name of a restaurant known as motorcycle meeting place (CH)

Eisenwaren - German word for hardware

Eis - German word for ice, also ice cream

entrecot - French for sirloin steak

etoile - French word for star, pl. etoiles

Euro - prefix for European

Fahrrad - German word for bicycle

ferme - French word for closed

formaggio - Italian word for cheese; often Parmesan

forno - Italian word for furnace, oven; al forno means baked

franc - French and Swiss unit of money

frei - German word for free, vacant; Zimmer Frei, room for rent

Furstentum - German word for principality; Furstentum Liechtenstein (FL)

Furst - German word for prince

Gasthaus - German word for inn

Gasthof - German word for inn

gelateria - Italian word for ice cream parlor

gelato - Italian word for ice cream

gemutlich - German word for comfortable

Gemutlichkeit - German word for coziness

Germania - Italian name for Germany

glace - French word for ice, ice cream

grosse - German adj., big

Hauser - German word for houses, plural of Haus

haut, haute - French adjective for high

Heidi - German woman's name; fictional Alpine story for children

heiss - German word for hot

Hochalpenstrasse - German for high Alpine road

Hochberghaus - German for high mountain house

hoch - German word for high

Hof - German word for court, court yard, yard, as in Gasthof

Hohe - German word for height

Hohenstrasse - German for high road

Hutte - German word for hut, a mountain refuge

insalata - Italian word for salad

Italia - (I) Italian word for Italy

Joch - German word for yoke, often applied to a pass

joli - French word for pretty

Kaiser Schmarrn - sweet Austrian dessert

Kalte - German word for cold (coldness)

Kaserne - German word for barracks

Kirche - German word for church

Konige - German word for kings

Konigschloss - German word for royal castle, palace

Kurort - German word for health resort, also see Aflenz Kurort

lac - French word for lake

lago - Italian word for lake

lavoro - Italian word for work, labor

le, les - French word for "the," singular and plural

linguini - pasta

lira - Italian unit of money

magno - Italian word for great; see Campo Carlo Magno

malhereusement - French word for unhappily

Mark - German unit of money

marmottes - mountain animal; Les Marmottes, a restaurant in La Thuile (I)

massif - a principle mountain

militaire - French word for military; see Route Militaire

mille - French word for thousand, see Les Mille Etoiles
Mitte - German word for middle, center, Stadtmitte means downtown
Montessori - Italian educator
Motorrad - German word for motorcycle; German motorcycle bi-monthly; plural is Motorrader
Moto Sport Schweiz - Swiss motorcycle weekly
Munchs - German motorcycle brand
Nasse - German word for wet
nazionale - Italian word for national
neu - German word for new
Novembre - Italian for November
ober - German word for upper
Osterreich - German name for Austria
ost - German word for east
ouvert - French word for open
parco - Italian word for park
parmesan - Italian variety of cheese
passo - Italian word for pass
Perrier - bottled water from France
Pinzgau - region (A) S of Salzburg
pomodoro - Italian word for tomato
ponte - Italian word for bridge
pre - prefix denoting priority
Prix - French word for prize
Puch - Austrian motorcycle
Rader - plural of Rad, German word for wheel
rifugio - Italian mountain refuge
ristorante - Italian word for restaurant
Rivella - a bottled soft drink in Switzerland
Romansch - the language of Graubunden (CH)
sacrario - Italian word for sanctuary, cemetery
Sattel - German word for saddle or pass
Schlucht - German word for gorge
Schweinshax'n - typical Austrian and Bavarian cut of pork
Schweiz - German word for Switzerland
See - German word for lake
Semmelknodel - an Austrian and Bavarian dumpling
Sinalco - soft drink in Switzerland
Sonne - German word for sun
Spezi - soft drink in Austria and Bavaria
Spitze - German word for top, tip, point; Edelweiss Spitze
Stadt - German word for city
Stausee - German word for reservoir created by a dam
Strasse - German word for road or street
sud - German word for south
Suisse - French name for Switzerland
Svizzera - Italian name for Switzerland

tagliatelli - pasta

Tal - German word for valley

telepherique - French word for cable car

terme - Italian word for hot spring

Tiroler - German for pertaining to Tirol

Toffel Strudel - an Austrian dessert

Toffler - Swiss German for motorcyclist

Toff - Swiss German word for motorcycle

Tofftreffpunkt - Swiss German for a motorcycle meeting place

Tor - German word for gate

tortellini - pasta

toutes - French word for all; toutes directions means all directions

trattoria - an Italian word for restaurant

tre - Italian word for three

Tyrol - English spelling of Tirol

Uberwachung - German word for oversee, supervise; Besonder Uberwachung means special supervision

Umleitung - German word for detour

und - German word for and

val - Italian, short for valle (valley)

valle - Italian for valley

Verkehrsburo - German for travel bureau

Versicherung - German word for insurance

viale - Italian word for avenue

vietato - Italian word for forbidden

vorder - German word for front

vous - French word for you

vue - French word for view

Wald - German word for forest

WC - common sign for toilet (Water Closet)

wechseln - German word for change, exchange

weiss - German word for white

Wienerschnitzel - cutlet (meat) Viennese style

Wurst - German word for sausage

Zimmer - German word for room; Zimmer Frei means room for rent

Index

Letters in parentheses indicate the country: (A) Austria; (CH) Switzerland; (D) Germany; (F) France; (FL) Liechtenstein; (I) Italy

Morbegno - town (I) Adda valley, N of Passo di San Marco 116, 118–119

Morgex - town (I) W of Aosta 70, 177

Morgins, Pas de - pass (CH)(F) from Rhone Valley at Monthey 76

Morzine - town (F) S of Lac Leman, Col du Joux Plane 77, 177

Mosses, Col des - pass (CH) NE of Lac Leman 57, 60, 66

Mulheim am der Ruhr 182

Munchen - German name for Munich, city (D) 17, 24, 133, 153, 183

Muotatal - valley (CH) SE Schwyz, Pragel Pass 44

Murau - town (A) S end of Solker Pass 173

Murtal - valley (A) SE of Salzburg 173

Mussolini - Fascist dictator of Italy 96

Mustair - town (CH) E of Ofen Pass 102

N Namlos - town (A) Tirol, S of Reutte 153

Nassereith - town (A) Tirol, S of Fern Pass 154–155

Nassfeld Pass - pass (I)(A) German name for Passo di Monte Croce Carnico; E of Cortina, S of Grossglockner 138–139, 168–169

Naters - town (CH) suburb of Brig, Rhone valley 67

Naturns - town (I) W of Merano 107

Neu St. Johann - town (CH) W of Liechtenstein 143

Neuchatel - town (CH) and lake, Lac du (CH) N of Lac Leman 63

Neuchatel, Lac du 63

Neuschwanstein - one of Ludwig's castles (D) near Fussen 153, 155, 158

Nice - city (F) 180

Nigra, Passo - pass (I) German name is Niger Pass; E Dolomites, from Karer Pass 132, 134

Nockalmstrasse - pass (A) toll, S of Turracher Hohe Pass 170, 173

Norway 179

Nova Levante - town (I) Dolomites, on Passo di Costalunga; German name is Welschnofen 134

Nova Ponente - town (I) W Dolomites, German name, Deutschnofen 134

Novena, Passo della - pass (CH) Italian name for Nufenen Pass 39

Nufenen Pass - (CH) W of Andermatt 38, 41, 90

Nurburgring - road race course (D) 182

Nurnberg - city (D) German name for Nuremberg 182

O Ober Bayern - German for Upper (southern) Bavaria 152

Oberalp Pass - (CH) E from Andermatt 31, 33, 40, 93–94, 96

Oberammergau - town (D) S of Munchen 152, 155

Oberaudorf - town (D) E of Munchen 160

Obergurgl - town (A) Timmels Joch 108

Oberjoch Pass - (D) W Deutsche Alpenstrasse 158

Obersalzberg - town (D) above Berchtesgaden 161

Obertauern - town (A) Radstadter Tauern Pass, S of Salzburg, 163, 172

Oberwald - town (CH) Goms, W of Furka Pass 39

Oberzeiring - town (A) N of Judenburg, S of Rottenmanner Tauern Pass 173

Occlini, Passo di - unpaved pass (I) German name is Grimm Joch; Dolomites from Passo di Lavaze 134

Ochsengarten - junction (A) of Haiming Joch and Kuhtai (hardly a town) 154, 178

Octodure, Hotel La Porte d' 65, 68

Ofen Pass - (CH) E of St. Moritz 100, 102

Oktoberfest - festival in Munchen in late September 17

Olang - town (I) German name for Valdaora; N of Dolomites, junction Furkel Sattel and Staller Sattel 137–138

Olten - city (CH) W of Zurich; Trimbach bei Olten, 55

Ora - town (I) in gorge of Adige, S of Bozen 133

Orsieres - town (CH) N of Col du Grand St. Bernard 69

Ortisei - town (I) German name is St. Ulrich; Grodnertal 134

Ossola, Val d' - valley (I) W of Locarno 90

Osterreichring - road race course (A) site of Austrian GP, E of Judenburg 173

Otz - town (A) W end of Kuhtai (some maps spell it Oetz) 154

P Padua - city (I) English name for Padova 133

Palade, Passo di - pass (I) Italian name for Gampen Joch, S of Merano 110

Palue - town (I) E of Passo de Fedaia, Dolomites, Sottoguda 128

Paradiso, Hotel 114–115

Pasterze - glacier (A) Grossglockner 172

Pennes, Passo di - pass (I) Italian name for Penser Joch, N of Bozen 110

NOTES:

NOTES:

Other Popular Books For Adventurers

Motorcycle Touring

Motorcycle Journeys Through New England
by Marty Berke

New England is undoubtedly one of the best areas of the United States for motorcycle touring. Owing to the great variety of terrain, roads in New England often seem haphazard in design and direction, but for motorcyclists seeking adventure travel through beautiful countryside, they are the stuff dream trips are made of.

This handy guide, perfectly sized to fit the map compartment of your tank bag, contains suggestions to help you find the best roads in six major riding regions. Altogether, Berke has carefully plotted 19 trips for you (that's less than 90 cents a trip), most of them taking one day to complete. Each trip is detailed by a map and route directions.

Berke brings the region alive with his quick wit and sharp eye for the off-beat, adding his recommendations for restaurants, diners, road-houses, places to stay, interesting places to visit, and the locations of emergency facilities. Berke's narrative gives you a handlebar view of this unique part of our country.

In addition, the book contains a listing of all major motorcycle dealers in New England. If you have mechanical trouble on the road, the motorcycle dealer listing alone is worth the price of the book.

Berke's interesting commentary and tips let you make the most of your travel time and budget. The trips are designed to accommodate various riding styles, from two-up travelers looking at every nook and cranny, to sport riders chasing more curves than a day's worth of hourglasses. Either way, this book makes it easy to find some great riding.

With over 25 years of riding experience and 15 years of world travel, Marty Berke is a knowledgeable host for your travels through New England.

Contents: • Introduction • Goin' Downeast (Maine, including Acadia National Park) • Cutting the White Mountain Notches (New Hampshire) • Closing the Green Mountain Gaps (Vermont) • Circumnavigating the Lakes (New York) • Cruisin' the Berkshires (Massachusetts) • The Southern Coastline (Connecticut and Rhode Island) • Motorcycle Service Facilities in New England • Index

Paper, 4 x 7-1/2 inches, 224 pages, 128 illustrations. **BERK $16.95**

MOTORCYCLE TOURING: An International Directory

The world's most complete planning guide to motorcycle vacations. . . now updated and expanded

If you love motorcycling, love to travel, and dream of combining those loves and heading off to exotic corners of the United States and the world, these are two books you must have. They provide a wealth of information and ideas on how to plan the riding vacation of a lifetime.

If you already own the 91/92 Directory, you'll find the 1993/94 Supplement to be a valuable update, with over 200 pages of new tours, tour operators, and rental companies, as well as updates on all the tours and operators in the 1991/92 Directory. There's even a completely new section that teaches you the tricks of transporting your motorcycle domestically or abroad.

If you don't own the 1991/92 Directory, this is your chance to see what you've been missing. With these two books you'll have descriptions of tours throughout the United States, as well as the Alps, Australia, Nepal, the Sahara, and scores of places in between. Prices, itineraries, departure dates, and other essential information are included in these easy-to-use resources. And, if you're just looking to rent a bike and ride on your own, you'll find complete and updated rental agency listings as well.

The 1993/94 Supplement is meant to be used in conjunction with the 1991/92 Directory. Only with both books will you have comprehensive, up-to-date information. No touring enthusiast should be without them.

Ordering:

1991/92 Directory: Paper, 360 pages, 5-1/2" x 8-1/2", 113 black and white photographs.
DIR $19.95

1993/94 Supplement: Softbound, 224 pages, 5-1/2" x 8-1/2", black and white photographs.
DIR93 $ 9.95

Special Offer! Save $5.00. *1991/92 Directory plus 1993/94 Supplement:* **SET2 $24.90**

Other Popular Books For Adventurers

●●●

Motorcycle Touring and Travel:
A Handbook of Travel by Motorcycle
by Bill Stermer,
*Editorial Director, **Rider** Magazine*

Here is THE handbook for anyone interested in travel by motorcycle, written by one of America's foremost riding journalists. Every aspect of planning and executing a trip by motorcycle is covered: picking the proper motorcycle and equipment, packing the right gear, dressing smart for various weather conditions, tips on accommodating co-riders and other motorcyclists, camping, safety — and just plain having fun.

Building on the success of his best-selling 1983 book, *Motorcycle Touring,* Bill Stermer has completely rewritten that standard of the touring community. *Motorcycle Touring and Travel* contains completely new information about tires, lubricants, suspension enhancements, routine maintenance and safety checks, clothing, and travel gear.

With over 30 years of riding experience and more than a dozen years testing and writing about motorcycles, Bill Stermer is the perfect guide for motorcycle travelers — novices and veterans alike. Even if you've been riding for 25 years, you are certain to learn something new from this book.

In the pointed words of noted touring authority and moto-journalist Clement Salvadori, **"Anyone who aspires to go traveling on a motorcycle, and who doesn't want to enjoy the character-building benefits of 'learning the hard way', is well-advised to read this book."**

Contents: • Introduction • Motorcycle Touring and Travel • Choosing Your Motorcycle • Accessories • Motorcycle Components • Motorcycle Apparel • The Tourer's Packing List • Planning a Tour • Co-Riders and Group Rides • Motorcycle Camping • Touring Security • Motorcycle Safety • Motorcycle Rallies and Clubs • Organized Tours • Foreign Travel • Index

Paper, 8-1/4 x 10-1/2 inches, 128 pages, 227 illustrations. **STER $24.95**

How to Tour Europe by Motorcycle
by Beverly Boe and Phil Philcox

Written in 1983, this book is now somewhat dated in its listings and specific references, but much of its advice and wisdom are timeless and remain valuable to anyone thinking of motorcycling in Europe. This book offers countless tips and suggestions on many important topics: planning your trip, insurance, licenses, renting or buying a motorcycle in Europe, camping and hosteling, where to go, touring and the weather, what to take and how to take it, things to know about Europe, how to speak "European-ese." With this book you can tap into Philcox and Boe's years of experience motorcycling in Europe and make your own trip more productive and enjoyable.

Paper, 5-1/2 x 8-1/2 inches, 135 pages, 80 illustrations. **PHIL $9.95**

Motorcycle Arizona!
by Frank Del Monte

Save time, be prepared, and avoid hassles with this compact guidebook on Arizona and the southwest. The book has five sections, each covering one of the five essential touring subjects: how to tour, where to tour, how to get there, where to stay, and what to see.

The first section covers general traveling tips, such as how to pack, what to wear, and how to get emergency service. This section also includes phone listings of important emergency services and visitor information bureaus throughout Arizona.

Sections 2 and 3 describe over 50 different motorcycling trips, ranging in length from one day to two weeks. Clear maps and detailed route descriptions make it easy to stay the course.

Section 4 provides complete listings of hotels and motels in all of the towns covered in the route descriptions, so that whether you're planning to end up in Bisbee or Tombstone, finding a place to stay is a snap.

The final section describes some of Arizona's most interesting attractions, ranging from the Petrified Forest in Holbrook to the Living Ghost Town in Jerome. Arizona offers some of the most breathtaking scenery in the country and this book ensures that you won't miss any of it.

Paper, 5-1/2 x 8-1/2 inches, 131 pages, 19 illustrations. **MCAZ $15.95**

Other Popular Books For Adventurers

● ●

The Best Roads of California
by Larry Blankenship

Read this amusing book before you even think of motorcycling in California. You'll learn the best this great state has to offer. Discover out-of-the-way back roads bursting with scenery, untouched by traffic and congestion. Gain new insight into old favorites like breathtaking Highway 1. For each route, this informative book covers the type of road, the road's best and worst stretches, the scenery, accurate driving times and distances, road and weather conditions, degree of difficulty, interesting and offbeat people and attractions, historical background, and more!

Paper, 5-1/4 x 8-1/2 inches, 161 pages, 10 illustrations. **BLNK $13.95**

Winging Through America
by Gary Shumway

Here is the tale to read if you've thought about getting on your bike and traveling cross-country. Author Gary Shumway presents an overview of the sights and sounds—uniquely American—that he encountered on his journey through America. During his marathon 24-day trip, Shumway touched all 48 of the continental states. You'll find appendices on recommended equipment and clothing, travel expenses, highway itineraries, overnight stops, telephone numbers for tourist bureaus by state, and suggested attractions by city. If you're in the mood for some serious pavement flogging, *Winging through America* may reinforce your conviction.

Paper, 5-1/2 x 8-1/2 inches, 172 pages, 46 b/w illustrations. **WINGA $10.95**

A Rider's Guidebook
by Bill Cooper

Here is a handy little book written by a man who has a lot to share and wanted to make life a little easier for other cycle enthusiasts. The book is filled with practical tips for making motorcycling more fun and enjoyable. Any one of Cooper's pearls of wisdom alone is worth the price of the book; together they provide a treasure chest of valuable information for riders at all levels of experience. You'll learn how to clean and protect your bike (aluminum and painted parts), how to stop brake squeal, how to stop annoying handlebar "buzz", care of face shields, bike security, making your seat more comfortable, riding in cold and hot weather. Even if you've been riding 30 years, you'll learn something from this book!

Paper, 5-1/2 x 8-1/2 inches, 28 pages, 16 illustrations. **COOP $4.95**

Motorcycle Sign Language
by Blane Kamp

If you're tired of having to pull over every time you want to communicate with your riding companions and you want to avoid buying expensive intercom systems, this handy book could be of great service. Using easy to follow illustrations, this book presents a set of basic hand signals used to communicate while driving.

Paper, 4 x 7 inches, 70 pages, approx 65 illustrations. **SIGN $5.95**

Travel Guides

On the Road USA
by Carroll Calkins, Editor

Liven up your next long distance freeway journey with this incredibly informative book of sights and attractions along America's interstates. This full-color, hardbound volume highlights over 1,200 things to see and do along the interstates and includes listings of parks, museums, towns, natural wonders, and much more. Virtually all of the places described in the book are 30 minutes or less from an interstate exit and clear, easy to follow directions accompany each description. If you plan on traveling on America's main roads, this book is sure to enrich your journey.

Hardbound, 10 x 10 inches, 238 pages, many color illustrations. **ORUSA $24.95**

National Forest Scenic Byways
by Beverly Magley

This book of America's most scenic drives was not written just for motorcyclists, but for any traveler who wants to take to the road in search of America's abundant beauty. Beverly Magley focuses on the system of Scenic Byways established by the USDA Forest Service to help travelers see our National Forests. There are now 156 National Forests in 44 states, offering a wide range of outdoor recreational activity.

For each Scenic Byway, Magley provides a general description of the road, its location and route numbers, special attractions found nearby, information about the travel season, information about camping and other services available, and contacts for further information. A tempting selection of photos and maps adds to the convenience and allure of this nicely organized, very useful book.

Paper, 6 x 9 inches, 240 pages, approx 175 illustrations. **BYWAY $9.95**

Other Popular Books For Adventurers

National Forest Scenic Byways II
by Beverly Magley

This companion to *Scenic Byways* covers 48 additional scenic byways in the National Forest system. From the multi-colored rock formations of Wyoming's Shoshone National Forest to the radiant reds, yellows and oranges of the autumn oaks in Virginia's George Washington National Forest, *Scenic Byways II*, like its predecessor, covers a variety of terrains throughout the country. New to this edition is an 8-page section containing vivid, full-color photographs of the stunning scenery you'll encounter on some of these roads.

Paper, 6 x 9 inches, 240 pages, many illustrations. **BY2 $11.95**

National Forest Scenic Byways Set
Why choose? Buy both books and save.
SET1 $20.00

Back Country Byways
by Stewart Green

For an informative book on the most scenic back roads in 11 Western States, consider *Back Country Byways* before you hit the pavement. Following the lead of the United States Forest Service, the Department of Interior's Bureau of Land Management developed a program called Back Country Byways to promote recreational driving opportunities on our nation's public land. Each route within the Byway system has been divided into four types, depending on the road, and the vehicle needed to drive it. Type I roads are paved or have an all-weather surface suitable for motorcycles. Type II roads are not paved but often have an improved gravel surface. Type III byways are unimproved dirt tracks and are negotiated best with dirt bikes, all-terrain and four-wheel drive vehicles. Type IV byways are trails that are managed for snowmobile, dirt bike, mountain bike, or ATV use. Moreover, the guide contains safety tips, information on camping, best and worst travel season for a particular route, notes on the natural habitat, topography, and wildlife. Experience America's back country byways.

Paper, 6 x 9 inches, 174 pages, 94 illustrations. **BCBY $9.95**

Arizona Scenic Drives
by Stewart Green

Arizona is a land of spectacular beauty, breathtaking panoramas, and unsurpassed natural wonders: the Grand Canyon, Petrified Forest, Monument Valley, and the lofty rim drives of Canyon de Chelly. In the spirit of *Scenic Byways* and *Scenic Byways II*, we recommend *Arizona Scenic Drives* to all travelers and motorcyclists waiting to explore the awe-inspiring scenery throughout Arizona.

This book highlights 39 of the most popular drives in the state, covering only a fraction of the many available. The roads included are sure to delight as you pass Hopi villages perched on mesa-tops, twist along the Coronado Trail, and explore the cacti gardens at Organ Pipe Cactus National Monument. Most of these road selections are paved two-lane highways; however, some are rough, unpaved backroads for the more adventurous types.

The book offers comprehensive route descriptions, including travel information on camping services, best seasons, special attractions, and historical points of interest. Detailed maps and black and white photos complement each description; eight pages of spectacular color photos taken along selected drives round out the book. When you are ready to explore the wondrous scenery in Arizona, let *Arizona Scenic Drives* show you the way.

Paper, 6 x 9 inches, 160 pages, maps & photos. **AZDR $11.95**

California Scenic Drives
by Stewart Green

Few states can match California for diverse scenery. Within its borders you'll find everything from redwood forests and snow-capped mountains to wind-swept deserts and sandy beaches. Discover the magic and beauty of the Golden State for yourself with this descriptive guide to 24 of California's most scenic drives. Each route listing comes with a detailed map and descriptions of natural wonders, scenic attractions, historic points of interest, and recreational opportunities. There's also plenty of information on camp sites, weather conditions, and visitor services. Lots of black and white photos, as well as an eight-page color section featuring spectacular pictures taken along selected drives.

Paper, 6 x 9 inches, 224 pages, some illustrations. **CADR $11.95**

Other Popular Books For Adventurers

Driving the Pacific Coast:
Oregon and Washington
by Kenn Oberrecht

This book is a comprehensive guide that covers 33 coastal towns along famed Highway 101. One element that makes this book stand out is its emphasis on recreational opportunities in relation to the sea; whether you like clam digging or tide exploration, this book can help you find the stretch of shoreline just right for you. The guide also includes information on history, lodging, camping, restaurants, shopping, and museums. It also lists telephone numbers for the US Forest Service, local Chambers of Commerce, and Visitor Centers, in case you want to obtain more detailed maps or information for the area. *Driving the Pacific Coast* is loaded with valuable material; however, you'll need good maps or a road atlas as a companion. Even though area maps are included in the book, they may prove to be inadequate for navigating smaller roads and towns beyond the scope of Highway 101.

Paper, 5-1/2 x 8-1/2 inches, 256 pages, 32 illustrations.   **DRPAC $12.95**

Journey to the High Southwest:
A Traveler's Guide (Third Edition)
by Robert L. Casey

If you like the history behind scenic landscapes and are a naturalist at heart, you'll be delighted with this book. Painstakingly researched and written, this guide contains a surplus of historical, geological, architectural, and travel information. Although the book is chock full of ideas and suggestions, it need not be overwhelming. If you take the time to absorb the material before mapping out your trip, you are bound to be happy with the results. Each chapter outlines a region with information about the area's terrain, national parks, and local towns. Also included is a chapter on "Staying There," which lists places to eat and sleep, information on tours, activities such as horseback riding and fishing, fairs, festivals, and special events. Finally, in the chapter on "Seeing," you'll find details on interesting roads to explore by car or motorcycle. *Journey To The High Southwest* is a veritable history book designed for the reader with travel in mind.

Paper, 7 x 9-1/4 inches, 476 pages, many illustrations.   **JHSW $18.95**

Country Roads Series

Here's delightful collection of guidebooks for the traveler yearning to explore the nooks and crannies of America's countryside. Use them to find the roads that might not exist on any maps, the points of interest that don't appear in any tour brochures, and the charming landscapes that have been discovered by only the most dedicated backroads explorers.

Written by travel writers with a passion for the small, the out-of-the-way, and the secluded, these books reveal nuggets of pastoral beauty and isolated, peaceful roads that will turn any motorcycle trip into a journey of rediscovery of America's rural heritage. There's plenty of picturesque, unspoiled beauty in this country, and with these guidebooks you'll be sure to find it.

Paper, 5-1/2 x 8-1/2 inches.

Country Roads of Hawaii
                                    CRHI $9.95
Country Roads of Illinois
                                    CRIL $9.95
Country Roads of Indiana
                                    CRIN $9.95
Country Roads of Kentucky
                                    CRKY $9.95
Country Roads of Massachusetts
                                    CRMA $9.95
Country Roads of Michigan
                                    CRMI $9.95
Country Roads of New Hampshire
                                    CRNH $9.95
Country Roads of New York
                                    CRNY $9.95
Country Roads of Ohio
                                    CROH $9.95
Country Roads of Oregon
                                    CROR $9.95
Country Roads of Pennsylvania
                                    CRPA $9.95
Country Roads of Quebec
                                    CRPQ $9.95
Country Roads of Vermont
                                    CRVT $9.95
Country Roads of Washington
                                    CRWA $9.95

Other Popular Books For Adventurers

The Alaska Highway
by Ron Dalby

The Alaska Highway, with its vast system of side roads, promises the greatest touring adventure remaining in North America. This book offers detailed, up-to-date information, while conveying the romance, the history, and adventure that await each visitor to the region. Each section covers what would be a comfortable day's drive, leaving plenty of time to take an occasional side trip. Moreover, the author includes mileages, distances to campgrounds and services, highway hazards, and key points of interest along the way.

This book is a valuable resource for planning a trip along the Alaska Highway; however, some of the more technical information about preparing one's vehicle for the journey neglects the motorcycle category. The author's main point, since Alaska's terrain can be rough and, at times, challenging, is to be certain your vehicle is in prime condition. Despite this shortcoming, you can still make use of the author's knowledge of the Alaska Highway for designing your own motorcycle tour. If you plan to travel the famed Alaska Highway, let this excellent book guide you.

Paper, 6 x 9 inches, 220 pages, maps & photos. **ALHW $15.95**

The Colorado Guide
by Bruce Caughey and Dean Winstanley

This is one of the most comprehensive guidebooks we've ever seen; the ultimate "visitor friendly" guide to Colorado. Arranged in six geographic regions, each region is divided into "destinations" which offer suggestions on all the things to see and do in the immediate area. Each destination contains a general introduction, including historical facts, and directions to the sights. Information is provided on major attractions, festivals and events, outdoor activities, sightseeing, lodging and camping, restaurants and services. There are gems in every chapter.

Don Long from The Denver Post says "The Colorado Guide very likely will come to be known as THE Colorado guidebook." Because Colorado offers such spectacular scenery and thousands of miles of superb roads, many people believe it offers the best motorcycling in the United States. If you are Colorado bound, make this book second on your list—right after your motorcycle. The book is thick and worth its weight in gold for motorcyclists looking for adventure and magnificent touring.

Paper, 6 x 9 inches, 628 pages, many maps, photos & illustrations. **COG $16.95**

The New Mexico Guide
by Charles L. Cadieux

This book is a fine publication for helping you find your way around the Southwestern state affectionately called the Land of Enchantment. Although the book was not written specifically from the vantage point of motorcycle touring, motorcyclists will want to pay particular attention to the sections on scenic drives. Here is where you will find intriguing and delightful places to explore. For example, in the chapter on Hispanic Highlands you'll find the Turquoise Trail which starts in Santa Fe and travels through historic Golden (site of the first gold rush west of the Mississippi), Cerillos (which once boasted 21 saloons), and Madrid (a coal-mining ghost town that is now home to a variety of artists). An extension of the Turquoise Trail takes you to the top of the Sandia Mountains. From that 10,000-foot perch you have a fantastic view of Albuquerque, and your horizon will stretch all the way to Mount Taylor, 75 miles to the west. In practical terms, this guide provides an overview of the best regional urban and rural attractions New Mexico has to offer its visitors. Each chapter provides a historical synopsis of the region and local highlights such as festivals and special events, outdoor activities, nearby attractions, night life, and accommodations.

Paper, 6 x 9 inches, 304 pages, many maps, photos, & illustrations. **NMG $15.95**

Hostelling Guide to North America
by Hostelling International

Anyone accustomed to traveling on a budget knows that hostels are an affordable and often educational way to explore the world. Rates run from $5.00 to $22.00 per night. This official guidebook, produced by Hostelling International, offers complete listings for all hostels located throughout the United States and Canada. It includes 200 detailed maps and illustrations and is indexed for easy reference. Use it the next time you're plotting a low-cost trek across America.

Paper, 4 x 8 inches, 368 pages, 200 illustrations. **HOSTEL $5.95**

Other Popular Books For Adventurers

- -

Obsessions Die Hard
by Ed Culberson

Since he was a teenager, Culberson had a fascination with the Pan American Highway System, which runs through North and South America. In his early forties he discovered motorcycling and decided to combine his two passions; he would drive his motorcycle from Alaska to Argentina. However, he didn't count on the Darien Gap, an 80-mile stretch in eastern Panama's Darien region and western Columbia, so densely filled with jungles, rain forests, rivers and swamps that travelers have long regarded it as impassable. The Darien Gap even has its own curse, aimed at trespassers who would challenge it. The dire warnings only strengthened Culberson's resolve and soon, crossing the Darien Gap became his obsession. This is the story of a man truly driven by a dream.

Paper, 6 x 9 inches, 258 pages, 20 illustrations.
CULB $11.95

Full Circle: Around the World with a Motorcycle and Sidecar
by Richard and Mopsa English

For Richard and Mopsa English, going on a long trip by motorcycle was something they had dreamed of for years. They decided to move back to their native London, work hard for 18 months and then take off on the trip of a lifetime on a 650cc Triumph Thunderbird.

Their 90,000-mile journey was not without incident and adventure. With humor and dogged persistence they survived political instability, mechanical breakdown, gunfire, and flood to return home after visiting sixty countries in four-and-a-half years. This book gives a fascinating account of their experiences, amply illustrated by black and white, and color photographs.

Hardbound, 7 x 9-1/2 inches, 216 pages, 120 illustrations.
FULL $29.95

Two Wheels to Adventure
by Danny Liska

Here's a story that challenges all motorcycle adventure yarns. Follow Danny Liska from Alaska to Argentina as he goes from adventure to adventure on his motorcycle. This book is packed with personal observations and anecdotes about the people he met and places he saw and contains thousands of photos collected on his journey. There is not a page of this mammoth book that doesn't contain something interesting. Danny's trip was extraordinary and the

book that resulted from it is an incredible publishing feat.

Hardbound, 6-1/2 x 9 inches, 759 pages, many illustrations.
LISKA $39.95

Blue Highways: A Journey into America
by William Least Heat Moon

When "Least Heat Moon" (a translation of the author's tribal name) lost his job at a college in western Missouri, a restlessness came over him. Tired of staying in the same place, he decided to go for what the Australian aboriginals call "a walk about." He bought a half-ton Ford van, packed up some necessities, including *Leaves of Grass* and Neihardt's *Black Elk Speaks,* and headed out to follow the tracks of his ancestors and write a book about America. But instead of looking for America on its main roads and highways, Least Heat Moon opted for finding an America which can only be found by traveling off the beaten path.

Join him as he visits little Post Office towns such as Nameless, Tennessee, Lookingglass, Oregon, the Cajun country of Louisiana and the drumlin hill near Palmyra, New York. He makes America seem new, in a special way.

Hardbound, 6-1/2 x 9-1/2 inches, 421 pages, approx 25 illustrations.
BLUE $24.95

Zen and the Art of Motorcycle Maintenance
by Robert M. Pirsig

One of the great books of our time, this story is not so much of Zen or even of motorcycles but of a man's attempt to find meaning in life. As Pirsig describes it, "The study of the art of motorcycle maintenance is really a miniature study of the art of rationality itself. Working on a motorcycle, working well, caring, is to become part of a process, to achieve an inner peace of mind. The motorcycle is primarily a mental phenomenon." This should already be on your bookshelf. If not, here's your chance.

Paper, 4-1/8 x 6-7/8 inches, 380 pages, no illustrations.
ZEN $5.95

Other Popular Books For Adventurers

Maps & Atlases

Fast Maps

When we first saw these maps, a cheer went up around the office. At last, a map maker realized that if maps are going to be used outside, they need to be protected from the weather. Fastmaps are the answer to every driver's prayers. They flip open and refold in a jiffy, are just the right size for a tank bag or side bag, and they are laminated for protection against the elements. The plastic coating accepts grease pencil or non-permanent marker for write-on, wipe off trip routing. Each colorful map features metro area and detailed street maps for both overall and close-up views. Also, an extensive index leads you to streets and important landmarks in the city of your choice. Get on track with colorful, convenient Fastmaps.

Paper, 4-1/2 x 11 inches, folded.

Albuquerque NM	FMALQ	$4.95
Atlanta GA	FMATL	$4.95
Austin TX	FMAUS	$4.95
Arizona	FMAZ	$4.95
Baltimore MD	FMBAL	$4.95
Bellevue WA	FMBEL	$4.95
Boston MA	FMBOS	$4.95
California North	FMNCA	$4.95
California South	FMSCA	$4.95
Cape Cod/Martha's Vineyard MA		
	FMCOD	$6.95
Chicago IL	FMCHI	$4.95
Washington DC	FMDC	$4.95
Denver CO	FMDEN	$4.95
Detroit MI	FMDET	$4.95
Dallas/Ft. Worth TX	FMDFW	$4.95
Florida/Disney World	FMFL	$4.95
Honolulu/Oahu HI	FMHON	$4.95
Houston TX	FMHOU	$4.95
Jacksonville FL	FMJAK	$4.95
Kansas City KS	FMKAN	$4.95
Los Angeles CA	FMLA	$4.95
LA Freeways CA	FMLAF	$4.95
Louisville KY	FMLOU	$4.95
Las Vegas NV	FMLV	$4.95
Memphis TN	FMMEM	$4.95
Miami FL	FMMIA	$4.95
Milwaukee WI	FMMIL	$4.95
Minneap./St Paul MN	FMMIN	$4.95
Minnesota	FMMN	$4.95
Nashville TN	FMNAS	$4.95
Norfolk/VA Beach VA	FMHRV	$4.95
New Orleans LA	FMNEO	$4.95
New Hampshire/Vermont		
	FMNHV	$4.95
New York City	FMNYC	$4.95
Orange County/Anaheim CA		
	FMORG	$4.95

Orlando FL	FMORL	$4.95
Pacific Coast	FMPAC	$4.95
Philadelphia PA	FMPHL	$4.95
Phoenix AZ	FMPHX	$4.95
Pittsburgh PA	FMPIT	$4.95
Portland OR	FMPOR	$4.95
Puerto Rico/San Juan	FMPR	$4.95
Sacramento CA	FMSAC	$4.95
Seattle WA	FMSEA	$4.95
San Antonio TX	FMSNA	$4.95
San Diego CA	FMSND	$4.95
San Francisco CA	FMSNF	$4.95
San Jose CA	FMSNJ	$4.95
Santa Fe/Taos NM	FMSNT	$6.95
St. Louis MO	FMSTL	$4.95
Tampa/St Petersburg FL	FMTAM	$4.95
Toronto ON	FMTOR	$4.95
Tucson AZ	FMTUC	$4.95
United States	FMUSA	$4.95
Vancouver/Victoria BC	FMVAN	$4.95
Washington State	FMWA	$4.95
Wisconsin	FMWI	$4.95

Michelin Road Atlas: Europe

If you are planning a driving trip in Europe, this is the Atlas to buy. It features large, easy-to-read maps of all countries in Eastern and Western Europe; dozens of helpful city maps; driving regulations in Europe; comprehensive index of placenames; a distance chart; and climate charts. The large format makes the atlas unsuitable for tank bags, so you'll want to buy folding maps of each area once you arrive in Europe.

Paper, 9-1/4 x 12 inches, 128 pages, many illustrations. **MICH $19.95**

Kummerly + Frey Maps

We've found Kummerly + Frey road maps to be the very best available in terms of both accuracy and thoroughness. The legends are printed in English, French, German, and Italian for ease of understanding, regardless of your native tongue. Each map folds up into a handy 5 x 9 inches and has a protective outer cover. The number next to the title indicates the scale.

Paper, 5 x 9 inches, folded.

Alpine Roads, 1:500,000	KFALP	$9.95
Austria, 1:500,000	KFAUS	$9.95
No. France, 1:600,000	KFFRN	$9.95
So. France, 1:600,000	KFFRS	$9.95
Rhone/Alps, 1:250,000	KFRA	$8.95
So. Germany, 1:500,000	KFGES	$9.95
Northern Italy, 1:500,000	KFITN	$8.95
Southern Italy, 1:500,000	KFITS	$8.95
Switzerland, 1:301,000	KFSWZ	$9.95